Daily
Poem Portraits

BY JAMES J. METCALFE

hanover house

GARDEN CITY, NEW YORK

BOOKS BY JAMES J. METCALFE

Daily Poem Portraits
Love Portraits
My Rosary of Rhymes
Poem Portraits
More Poem Portraits
Garden in My Heart
James J. Metcalfe's Poems for Children

LIBRARY OF CONGRESS CATALOG CARD NUMBER: 54–9847

Contents by Subject

[4]

[5]

The Seasons

The Year Is a Day

Miscellaneous

Dedication

I dedicate this calendar . . . Of rhythm and of rhyme . . . To all the souls who honor God . . . Throughout their earthly time . . . Who live their lives unselfishly . . . And do the best they can . . . To serve the flag, their family . . . And every fellow man . . . Who do not flinch in time of stress . . . Or falter in their stride . . . But who go forward in the faith . . . That God is at their side . . . May every morning, noon, and eve . . . Of each succeeding day . . . Be filled with hope and happiness . . . And peace along their way . . . I pray this calendar will mark . . . Another fruitful year . . . For all the gentle souls who are . . . Devoted and sincere.

Foreword

James J. Metcalfe's daily column of verse, now in its tenth year of syndication, is familiar to newspaper readers from coast to coast.

The popularity of his writings in terms of newspaper circulation is rivalled in no small degree by the constant demand for his poems in book form. Among his published works are two books of his diversified writings—*Poem Portraits* and *More Poem Portraits;* a volume devoted exclusively to love—*Love Portraits;* two compilations of religious thoughts and prayers—*Garden in My Heart* and *My Rosary of Rhymes,* and his delightful rhymes for youngsters—*Poems for Children.*

Now he brings you his newest and most unique book—*Daily Poem Portraits.* It gives you a thought for the day—not just today—but for every day throughout the year. Teeming with love, prayer, friendship, and philosophy, it offers a calendar for your heart. You will find it a year to read and remember, and to read again in happy or lonely hours.

Journalist, lawyer, and former F.B.I. agent, Jim Metcalfe is just your fellow man who wants to share with you in rhyme and rhythm his thoughts and dreams, so much like yours.

The Publishers

A happy and prosperous New Year is always a wish well meant—but the more important thing about New Year's is that we are making another start. It is our traditional opportunity for new resolutions, and to try earnestly to keep them. However poorly we have done, however discouraged we may be, we should lift our hearts to God and thank Him for letting us begin another year on earth. The past is over now, and may this be—

A BLESSED YEAR

God bless you on this New Year's Day . . . And all throughout the year . . . And may it be your happiest . . . With every moment dear . . . Each moment of the days and weeks . . . And every month in store . . . With progress toward whatever goal . . . Your heart is striving for . . . Whatever days have disappeared . . . The past is over now . . . And all the future hinges on . . . How well you keep your vow . . . Your New Year's resolution and . . . Your eagerness to win . . . Depend on how sincerely and . . . How bravely you begin . . . And so as this new calendar . . . Is joyously begun . . . May God be with you every day . . . Until the year is done.

There is no New Year's resolution that will be treasured more by the one you love than to promise your utmost devotion, your efforts, your hopes and your dreams. It is the gift of your heart for all the pages of the calendar—the months, the weeks and the days—as you whisper to your beloved—

THIS YEAR FOR YOU

I offer you this new year, love . . . With all that I can give . . . To bring you happiness each day . . . And moment that you live . . . I offer everything I have . . . And I may come to own . . . As it may help to please your heart . . . For you, and you alone . . . With all my wishes in the well . . . And all my hopes for you . . . And every prayer that I repeat . . . To make your dreams come true . . . And as each sunset disappears . . . Before another dawn . . . May memories grow sweeter through . . . The hours that are gone . . . I offer you this new year, love . . . Wherever you may be . . . And all I ask you in return . . . Is just to think of me.

Wouldn't this be a wonderful time to go to Florida; that is, if you are living in the cold, shivering North? Just cup your ear, and you can hear—

FLORIDA CALLING

It's time to go to Florida . . . And have a good vacation . . . If you can spend the money and . . . You need the relaxation . . . To swim and frolic in the sun . . . To cast or troll for fishes . . . To dance beneath a sky of stars . . . And dine on dainty dishes . . . There are the trains and planes each day . . . That take you in a hurry . . . In comfort and in luxury . . . Away from every worry . . . Miami and Miami Beach . . . Key West and many places . . . Where you will have a happy time . . . And see familiar faces . . . But if you have to punch the clock . . . To keep your business going . . . Then just forget the sunshine and . . . Remember it is snowing.

"Give us this day our daily bread." This is a most beautiful part of The Lord's Prayer. The word "bread" does not mean a mere loaf from the oven. It signifies our entire bodily sustenance, be it bread or meat, fish, vegetable or milk. It is our food and drink. It is the harvest from our fields, the milk and butter from our cows, the meat from our cattle and hogs and sheep. For this, our daily bread, we think of and give thanks to our—

FARM FOLKS

I like to watch the farmer at . . . The turning of his plow . . . His tractor or his horses and . . . The sweat upon his brow . . . I like to watch him milk the cows . . . And feed the pigs and hogs . . . And wield his ax above the ground . . . To cut some burning logs . . . To see his wife come out the door . . . And tend the chicken flock . . . Prepare the meals and sweep and scrub . . . And sew a Sunday frock . . . There is no finer family . . . Or one of greater worth . . . Than those endearing folks who make . . . Their living from the earth . . . Their harvest is the healthy yield . . . That keeps the world alive . . . And theirs should be a rich reward . . . On which they justly thrive.

How tall are you? How tall are those around you? Do you feel small by comparison? Then you may be thinking in terms of physical measurement, from head to toe. You have forgotten or overlooked the more important measurement of life. It is not your body that counts, it is not your physical stamina—it is the value of your contribution to the world and to your fellow man. It is your—

HUMAN HEIGHT

What is the truthful measurement . . . Of human height today?
. . . Is it the inches and the feet? . . . The pounds that people
weigh? . . . No, it is not the size or weight . . . Of bodies on this
earth . . . But only what a woman or . . . A man is really worth
. . . It is the height of character . . . The length of honesty . . .
The width of friendship and the depth . . . Of their sincerity . . .
It is the nobleness that counts . . . The daily sacrifice . . . The
charity to serve the world . . . And pay a higher price . . . It is
that willingness to live . . . For others day and night . . . That
weighs the value of a soul . . . And measures human height.

January 6

There is no such word as "good-by" in the language of love. Those in love are together always, even when one of them is away for a while. They are together in their hearts, as each whispers to the other: You are—

MY EVERYTHING

I say good night to you, my love . . . But never, dear, good-by
. . . Because you linger in the stars . . . That decorate the sky . . .
You linger in the moon that fades . . . And in my memory . . .
And in my every happy dream . . . You are a part of me . . . I
could not live without your heart . . . Or ever reach my goal . . .
Unless I touched the beauty and . . . The wisdom of your soul
. . . You are the only hope I have . . . The only song I sing . . .
You are the promise of my life . . . You are my everything.

When you say a prayer, do you pray with your heart or your lips? Is it lip service, or does it come from within you? Do you mean it? Or do you go to church on Sunday, in your latest-style clothes, merely to make an impression on those around you? It may please your neighbors, but as far as God is concerned—

THE HEART MUST PRAY

The tongue and lips may speak of God . . . With all that they can say . . . But more importantly in life . . . The human heart must pray . . . A prayer to God must be sincere . . . It must be truly meant . . . Because there is no prayer fulfilled . . . Except to that extent . . . It must be really from the heart . . . As much as it can be . . . For only in the heart itself . . . Is there sincerity . . . So let us give ourselves to God . . . As fully as we can . . . When we ask favors for ourselves . . . Or for our fellow man . . . Let us be honest in our words . . . And make our meaning clear . . . So every prayer that we recite . . . Is fervent and sincere.

In our youth a day seems like a year, but as we grow older and older we have the feeling that each year passes more swiftly, until eventually it appears that a whole year is not much more than just another day—from dawn to dusk. Yesterday is last year, tomorrow is next year, today is this year. And so as we are in the month of January, let us consider this the—

DAWN OF THE YEAR

The month of January is . . . The dawning of the year . . . That starts another record book . . . With pages white and clear . . . It brings the chance to start anew . . . And hope for better breaks . . . While striving hard to profit from . . . Our previous mistakes . . . It is the dawn of brighter dreams . . . We pray will all come true . . . With happiness and real success . . . Beneath a sky of blue . . . So let us all begin again . . . As ably as we can . . . To live our lives for God and for . . . Our every fellow man . . . And let us not be negligent . . . Or tardy on our way . . . That no tomorrow may become . . . A wasted yesterday.

An occasional trip to the photographer augments the family's official album of how they looked their best that day, but nothing is so realistic or more fun than just the ordinary, informal—

SNAPSHOT

A snapshot is a picture of . . . Yourself or family . . . When life is quite relaxed, and time . . . Is passing pleasantly . . . It is a sudden likeness of . . . The way you looked and felt . . . Regardless of your hair-do or . . . The tightness of your belt . . . It shows your children as they are . . . Without their special dress . . . But honestly according to . . . Their style of happiness . . . It is a better picture than . . . The formal photograph . . . Of eyes that gaze with dignity . . . Or little lips that laugh . . . A snapshot is the picture of . . . Your quite informal pose . . . Without the need of studio . . . Or powder on your nose.

There have been many friends in my life, as there have been in yours. As you know, some are for today, and some are for ever. Sooner or later you find them out. They are faithful or false. They deserve you or desert you. But when a friend stays with you through thick and thin, when he will never let you down—you know that he is your and—

MY CHERISHED FRIEND

My friend is one who speaks to me . . . And takes the time to write . . . Who has a thought to spare for me . . . Whatever day or night . . . Who comforts me and wants to make . . . My worry his concern . . . Who does a favor but expects . . . No favor in return . . . The one who knows the faults I have . . . But does not criticize . . . And who is always at my side . . . To help and sympathize . . . He is the brother of my soul . . . Forever good and kind . . . And he is first and foremost in . . . My grateful heart and mind . . . My friend is one who keeps me in . . . His every memory . . . And now and then will turn to God . . . And say a prayer for me.

Can you ever do enough for the one you love? No, because no matter how much you do, in your heart you want to bestow even more. Your happiness depends upon the joy and contentment of your beloved. You want to protect and cherish, provide and comfort, encourage and help, and after that—

WHAT FAVOR, LOVE?

What can I do for you, my love? . . . What favor large or small? . . . You surely know that I would do . . . Just anything at all . . . How can I make you happier? . . . What treasure do you seek? . . . I want to serve you day and night . . . Whatever month or week . . . I want to soothe and comfort you . . . In trouble and in pain . . . I want to play the part of your . . . Umbrella in the rain . . . Give me your confidence, my love . . . Believe in what I say . . . Let me defend you from all fear . . . And take your tears away . . . You will not owe me anything . . . Your conscience will be free . . . I only hope your heart will care . . . A little bit for me.

Men dominate the world, especially the business world, but it has been said many times that behind every successful man there is usually a woman—his wife. Have you ever thought of your—

WIFE AS A SALESMAN

There are a million salesmen who . . . Are experts in their field . . . And promptly take the credit for . . . Their labor and its yield . . . But where would many of them be . . . Without the helpful wife . . . Who does so much to counsel and . . . Promote his selling life? . . . Who dresses him in stylish clothes . . . And gives him cash to spend . . . And entertains the buyer or . . . Some other business friend? . . . So many times it is her charm . . . And smiling sacrifice . . . That gets the larger order at . . . The very highest price . . . She is the girl behind the stage . . . Prepared with every cue . . . To help her salesman-husband and . . . To make their dreams come true.

What is more gratifying or heart warming than those first scrawls and scribbles from the hand of your own little boy or girl, in a note that is sent just to you? That envelope is not directed to your house number and the name of your street—it is addressed to your heart. And as you envision the loving effort of those small fingers to let you know how much you mean, you treasure that—

FIRST LETTER

Today I got a letter cute . . . That I will always keep . . . And I will read it every night . . . Before I go to sleep . . . The first one that my daughter wrote . . . And signed and mailed to me . . . So childishly and naturally . . . And, oh, so lovingly . . . God bless my own Kristina dear . . . God bless my Snuggle-Bear . . . For all those minutes of her time . . . That she could hardly spare . . . The time she needs for schoolwork and . . . Her music and her play . . . And all the other things to do . . . That occupy her day . . . Her letter is my treasure and . . . I hope there will be more . . . Wherever mailmen follow me . . . To knock upon my door.

As we go through life, we may be rich or poor, and we may think we are lucky or unlucky. These things do not really matter. The important thing is, what do we accomplish? If we do anything worth while, it can be only by the grace of God, and this is what we should realize in all humility. Without His grace, we are as nothing. So let us say each day—

GIVE ME YOUR GRACE

Dear God, I want to live for You . . . In thought and word and deed . . . So I may ask for comfort in . . . The hour of my need . . . I want to gain Your promise and . . . The blessings You bestow . . . But, oh, my flesh is feeble and . . . My progress is so slow . . . I have the common weaknesses . . . Of selfishness and pride . . . And other faults that are so hard . . . For me to put aside . . . Please give me grace to hear Your word . . . And glimpse Your guiding light . . . That I may walk with You each day . . . And not be lost at night . . . Or else it may be years before . . . My spirit is resigned . . . And possibly Your path will be . . . The one I never find.

However long we are married, we should never become complacent to the point of taking our spouse for granted. Our devotion and kindness may reflect our gratitude, but at least occasionally our loved one wants to hear those words: I give you—

MY LOVING THANKS

I write this letter not to ask . . . For anything from you . . . But just to thank you for yourself . . . And everything you do . . . To thank you for your goodness and . . . The beauty of your heart . . . And for the promise you pronounced . . . That we will never part . . . I know that you will keep it, dear . . . As surely as I say . . . My love is yours to have and hold . . . Forever and a day . . . I love you for the way you smile . . . And every word you speak . . . And for the softness of your lips . . . When they caress my cheek . . . I write this letter only to . . . Repeat these words to you . . . I thank you and I love you and . . . I will be always true.

We have our special friends, with whom we keep in constant touch. Then there are those we see quite often, and those just now and then. But whether here and there, or always and everywhere, do we ever think of what they mean to us? Do we thank them for being our friends—for their companionship, their encouragement and consolation? Why not send them a card today, or lift the phone and say—

THANK YOU, FRIEND

This message is the one that I . . . Have always meant to send . . . A little note of thanks to you . . . Because you are my friend . . . It is no masterpiece of words . . . In prose or poetry . . . But just the heartfelt gratitude . . . To you, my friend, from me . . . My gratitude for every dream . . . And hope that you have shared . . . And every way your deeds have shown . . . That you have always cared . . . For all your praise and sympathy . . . Your pride in my success . . . And every way that you have helped . . . To bring me happiness . . . A friend like you is hard to find . . . A friend so good and true . . . And there are not sufficient thanks . . . That I can say to you.

[16]

As a rule, children (and canines too) have no love for the dog-catcher. For that matter, few dogcatchers enjoy their own occupation. But people, and especially youngsters, seldom realize that someone must round up the strays, to provide shelter for God's neglected animals, or prevent the spread of disease that could be fatal to dog or human. So let us consider and appreciate the problems of the—

DOGCATCHER

His task is not a pleasant one . . . For he must look around . . .
To pick up every pooch that he . . . Can put into the pound . . .
If he has any love for dogs . . . His heart must sympathize . . .
With those unwanted animals . . . Of every age and size . . . The
spaniel and the terrier . . . The collie and the bull . . . The shep-
herd and the poodle with . . . Aristocratic wool . . . But now and
then he is repaid . . . And he is filled with joy . . . To see a
puppy snuggle up . . . To some young girl or boy . . . For it will
have a happy home . . . With all the best of care . . . And freedom and affection and . . . With pleasure everywhere.

cold

Cold? Sure, what do you expect? It's winter now. But it won't be too long before spring will be here again, and then a long, lazy summer, and a dreamy autumn. Be patient. The seasons come and go. Right now—

IT'S WINTERTIME

The temperature is down tonight . . . The snow is at our door
. . . And Mr. Weatherman predicts . . . That there will be some
more . . . It may become a whole lot worse . . . With ice and
slush and sleet . . . Until it is too difficult . . . To navigate the
street . . . But after all, it's wintertime . . . And that is part of it
. . . So why should anyone complain . . . Or have a sudden fit?
. . . It cannot last forever, and . . . The morning will arrive . . .
When all the leaves and flowers and . . . The grass will be alive
. . . It's winter in the window when . . . The drapes and curtains
part . . . But there is always room enough . . . For springtime in
the heart.

Our thoughts provoke our actions, and only as we think right, can we live right. The same is true of love. Our display of affection means nothing unless we really think and feel the words we say, the promises we make. True love is sincerity, not flattery—it is the voice of the heart. So may each soul be guided, as he or she may say these are—

MY THOUGHTS ✓

My thoughts of you are in the sun . . . That lights your happy day . . . And in the silver stars that shine . . . When dusk has slipped away . . . They follow you from door to door . . . Where-ever you may be . . . And they are part of every hope . . . And every memory . . . Each month of every season and . . . Each hour of the week . . . My thoughts reflect the sentiments . . . My loving heart would speak . . . And when the rain is falling and . . . A tear is in your eye . . . My thoughts are in your loneliness . . . And in your every sigh . . . My thoughts are with you constantly . . . Because I love you, dear . . . For being so unselfishly . . . Devoted and sincere.

Whatever our party affiliation, when the national election is over we should all join hands and strive for our mutual welfare. We may find fault with the new administration as time goes on, but we ought to put aside the bitterness of political campaigns when the Chief Executive takes his oath to defend the Constitution, and give full support to our—

NEW PRESIDENT

God bless our President on his . . . Inauguration Day . . . And help him guide our country on . . . Its freedom-loving way . . . May he provide the leadership . . . For true and lasting peace . . . And do the best he can to make . . . Prosperity increase . . . Of course he cannot do it all . . . A lot of it depends . . . On whether those in Congress are . . . His enemies or friends . . . But may his wisdom be the best . . . And may God help him on . . . To bring the whole United States . . . A brighter, better dawn . . . God bless our chosen President . . . And give him strength to do . . . The duties of his office and . . . To see our struggle through.

God gave us life and the free will to keep ourselves and each other alive as long as He allows. He commands us, "Thou shalt not kill." In this, as in everything, we need His grace. So let us say a—

PRAYER FOR SURVIVAL

Dear God, as we are creatures You . . . Allow to be alive . . . Give us the wisdom and the strength . . . And courage to survive . . . The strength and courage to survive . . . If there must be a war . . . And wisdom that will win the world . . . To peace for evermore . . . Let not Your temple on this earth . . . Be crumbled into dust . . . Let not the steeple of our faith . . . Be sepulchered in rust . . . Teach us to teach our enemy . . . To be a brother true . . . That we may pray together with . . . Our praise and thanks to You . . . Help us to help each other through . . . Our struggle and our strife . . . And grant that we survive, dear God . . . In Your eternal life.

All children love the soda fountain—its sundaes with whipped cream and cherry or nuts, the malted or milk shake, the fizzing soda —chocolate, vanilla, strawberry. It's fun to go there but it's even better when you can have those treats right in your own home. At least we thought so when we got us a—

DRINK-MIXER

We got a mixer for our drinks . . . To make the children stout . . . And so when they were thirsty they . . . Would not be running out . . . And Daddy would not have to make . . . A special trip at night . . . To get the milk and malted shakes . . . That please the appetite . . . Of course the youngsters love it and . . . They seem to gain in weight . . . And I am glad and grateful that . . . I need not go out late . . . But now we have to buy ice cream . . . And all the mixes too . . . In quantities much greater than . . . We ever had to do . . . And while it is a happy and . . . A healthy novelty . . . It seems to be distracting to . . . Our home economy.

Perhaps more than anything else, a kiss personifies love. It is our outward sign of affection, respect and reverence. It is the warm greeting to a spouse, a relative, a child or a dear friend. Sometimes one kiss can say more than all the words ever spoken or written—or so it seems. Now and then, to the one we love most, we ought to say thank you for—

YOUR LOVING KISS

I loved you when I met you, dear . . . I loved you when we kissed . . . And when I had to be alone . . . You were the one I missed . . . I cherished you with all my heart . . . And every thought sincere . . . In summer, spring and winter and . . . In autumn every year . . . And now so many calendars . . . Have put the years away . . . Yet everything is just the same . . . As it was yesterday . . . Unless perhaps it is more sweet . . . And wonderful to me . . . Because of you in each embrace . . . And every memory . . . Because our life together, love . . . Is still the perfect bliss . . . That sealed our youthful promise in . . . That first and lasting kiss.

Life is happy and exciting as it moves at a rapid pace, but there is an inner joy—a peace and contentment—that is nowhere to be found at Times Square, or Hollywood and Vine. It's just around the corner, on that little—

SIDE STREET

The downtown street is interesting . . . The busy thoroughfare . . . Where buses roll and people stroll . . . With shopping everywhere . . . And some may like to join the crowd . . . That rushes to a sale . . . And some may stand in line to see . . . Some stage or movie tale . . . But I prefer the side street small . . . Where life is standing still . . . Except for friendly folks who call . . . Across the window sill . . . Except for childish laughter and . . . The sound of trikes and bikes . . . The mailman, milkman, and the dogs . . . That everybody likes . . . I love the little side street where . . . The struggle seems to cease . . . And where the sidewalk is a path . . . To happiness and peace.

Your day is a busy one, in the office or at home. Yet, how many times does your mind wander off into space? And what about moments of actual idleness, when you do not have to think of anyone or anything in particular? Why not think of a friend, perhaps someone long neglected or sort of forgotten, whom you might be able to help? There is nothing more cherished than just a—

FRIENDLY THOUGHT

What can be nicer in this world . . . Than just a friendly thought . . . According to the common love . . . That all of us are taught? . . . The friendly thought that is expressed . . . By mail or telephone . . . Especially when someone is . . . In trouble or alone . . . Why not remember someone now . . . In sickness or distress? . . . It takes so little of our time . . . To scatter happiness . . . A friendly word, a greeting card . . . A finger on the bell . . . A brief hello, a kindly smile . . . And "just to wish you well" . . . If everyone on earth would have . . . A friendly thought today . . . The world could pack its troubles up . . . And put them all away.

Any doctor will tell you that a good, solid breakfast is the best way to start out the day. Some folks skip it or just gulp a cup of coffee or a bit of orange juice—perhaps gobble a slice of toast. They figure to make it up at lunch and dinner, or maybe they are on a diet. But even a baby can tell you that nothing is more healthy for you than a real good—

BREAKFAST

Doctors say that breakfast is . . . Important every day . . . Gives you all that energy . . . To start you on your way . . . You should eat a cereal . . . Drink some fruity juice . . . And consume an egg or two . . . To be of better use . . . In my own experience . . . That is tops in truth . . . Breakfast builds a baby and . . . It helps you keep your youth . . . Eat your breakfast every day . . . Grab it on the run . . . But be sure you swallow it . . . In time for work and fun . . . After breakfast there is lunch . . . And then the evening meal . . . But breakfast helps you most of all . . . The way you want to feel.

The marriage ring makes love a sacred thing, and once those vows have been exchanged, the daily words from spouse to spouse should be—

MY LOVE FOREVER

I give my love to you today . . . As much as I can say it . . . I offer you my faithful heart . . . As truly as you weigh it . . . As truly as you promise, dear . . . For all eternity . . . That every day and week and month . . . You will belong to me . . . As much as you are mine, my love . . . I will be yours forever . . . And though the stars may disappear . . . I will not leave you ever . . . I want you more than I can write . . . In words for you to read . . . And more than I can whisper, dear . . . How much your heart I need . . . I offer you my happiness . . . But never any sorrow . . . For every moment of today . . . And every new tomorrow.

"Blessed are the meek, for they shall possess the earth." Who are we, except as God gave us life and endowed us with our abilities? What right have we to be proud? Any credit we receive in life belongs to God, and we ought to pass it on to Him. "Pride goeth before a fall." Let us remember that our every talent is a gift from our Creator, and let us say a—

PRAYER FOR HUMILITY

Dear God, let me remember now . . . That I belong to you . . . Give me humility of heart . . . In everything I do . . . Remind me in the worldly joys . . . For which my heart may yearn . . . I am but dust, and unto dust . . . Some day I must return . . . Allow me not to gather wealth . . . Or popularity . . . Unless I credit You, my God . . . In all humility . . . Unless I give whatever gain . . . As much as I can share . . . With my community and all . . . Your people everywhere . . . For all I am and all I have . . . Belong to You alone . . . And all I hope and ask and pray . . . Is just to be Your own.

Most of us like to be independent. We dislike working for some-one else, and we dream of the day when we can be the boss and run our own business. But there are just so many individuals who are qualified to direct and supervise the commerce of the world, and we may not be among them. So let us be careful about—

BEING IN BUSINESS

Most people wish that they could be . . . In business for them-selves . . . In some profession or a store . . . With goods upon their shelves . . . And that is very well indeed . . . If they are qualified . . . With knowledge and ability . . . That have to be applied . . . But some will try it anyway . . . Because they want to be . . . The mighty masters of their own . . . Financial destiny . . . Perhaps they feel important in . . . A business of their own . . . Or they resent direction and . . . They want to work alone . . . But when the chips are down and when . . . They take a heavy loss . . . They find there is no happiness . . . In being their own boss.

Yesterday we were talking about the possibility of success in busi-ness. But what really is success? It is not to be found in terms of wealth or fame. It is a matter of how one serves his fellow man. Only that is the measure of—

YOUR REAL SUCCESS

What are your chances in this life . . . To reach a real success? . . . What is your opportunity . . . For perfect happiness? . . . The odds may be a thousand or . . . A million unto one . . . And you may never live to see . . . The rising of your sun . . . Your chance in life depends upon . . . The wisdom of your goal . . . And whether you are striving with . . . Your brain or with your soul . . . Is all your interest in yourself . . . And reaching for the moon? . . . Then yours must be a selfish and . . . At last a fateful tune . . . But if you live for others and . . . You truly try to serve . . . You will receive the real success . . . You honestly deserve.

When in your youthful days you have an "understanding" with someone—or at least you think you do—and when that someone walks out of your life, it can be mighty heartbreaking. You have no real claim to press, and all you can say is—

I WISH SOMEHOW

You loved me once with all your heart . . . And once I loved you too . . . And in our hearts we promised then . . . To be forever true . . . No, there was no engagement ring . . . Or any sacred vow . . . Although I wish with all my soul . . . There would have been somehow . . . And yet your loving influence . . . Has never left my heart . . . And I believe that in a way . . . We still are not apart . . . We had an understanding that . . . Reflected in your eyes . . . As beautiful as sunshine and . . . The stars around the skies . . . But you may not remember it . . . And I shall never blame you . . . And though the world be curious . . . I will not ever name you.

Of course, bobby-pins are not a penny a pound, and my dear wife would never intentionally throw anything away. She is very thrifty but she can be somewhat careless about her possessions. She wouldn't do it with mink or diamonds (if we could afford them) but she sure can give me a headache when it comes to—

HER BOBBY-PINS

In every room throughout the house . . . That I am walking in . . . I never fail to come across . . . Another bobby-pin . . . In living room and dining room . . . And on the bedroom floor . . . In bathroom, study, on the porch . . . I find them by the score . . . Apparently my darling wife . . . Is tossing them around . . . Like bobby-pins are only worth . . . A penny for a pound . . . I pick them up and lay them down . . . Where she can see each pin . . . But, all in all, it is a game . . . I cannot hope to win . . . Each day I wander through the house . . . And find them everywhere . . . My wife may put them on her head . . . But they get in my hair.

*Some folks call it the ground hog, others say it's the woodchuck,
but the only shadow of a doubt is whether that animal will see its
shadow, to predict the season on—*

GROUND-HOG DAY

Each February 2nd is . . . That special Ground-Hog Day . . .
When woodchucks scurry back to bed . . . Or stay outside and play
. . . They break the ground and look around . . . With curiosity
. . . And spring is here again unless . . . Their shadows they can
see . . . But if the sun is shining and . . . The shadow is in sight
. . . Six weeks of winter still must cast . . . Their cold on day
and night . . . It is an old tradition and . . . Some people watch
each year . . . To figure out the weather when . . . The woodchucks reappear . . . The ground hog heralds spring again . . . Or
it predicts more snow . . . And maybe you believe it but . . . It
isn't really so.

*Friends come and go but the true friend remains forever. He is
there to comfort and console, to share our happiness, to encourage
and inspire us. He does not judge or condemn. He believes in us,
and all he asks in return is our faithfulness to him. The true friendship is a flower whose bloom never fades, and that is why I like to
think of my friends as—*

MY PERENNIALS

All my friendships are like flowers . . . Fragrant through the
passing hours . . . Like a satisfying potion . . . Of the deepest of
devotion . . . They mean more than any weather . . . As we live
our lives together . . . They are blossoms in the morning . . .
With their virtues so adorning . . . Love and truth and lasting
beauty . . . And a faithfulness to duty . . . All my friends of every
station . . . Are my constant inspiration . . . They are solace in
my sorrow . . . And my hope for each tomorrow . . . And though
others try to hurt me . . . And my lucky stars desert me . . . They
will never leave me—never . . . Even when I leave forever.

[25]

Sunday is God's day. Of course, every day belongs to Him but Sunday is something special. It is the day we may rest from our labors, with more time for worship and holy contemplation. Still, Sunday is no reason or excuse to forget God the rest of the week. So let us tell Him: I adore You and I thank You, especially (not just)—

ON SUNDAY, GOD

On Sunday, God, I give myself . . . And all my thoughts to You . . . With every worthy deed on earth . . . I ever try to do . . . I offer You my suffering . . . My labor and this prayer . . . That You will be a friend to me . . . And keep me in Your care . . . I turn to You on Sunday, God . . . Because it is Your day . . . And all the world should honor You . . . In every special way . . . I know I should be conscious of . . . Each day of every week . . . To worship You and ask You for . . . The favors that I seek . . . But when the week is passing by . . . I casually forget . . . And then on Sunday, God, my soul . . . Is filled with deep regret.

The lighted candle on an altar, in the window of a home, or on the dinner table is a symbol of faith and our warmth of feeling. So also should be our—

CANDLE OF LOVE

Dear one, the love I have for you . . . Is like a candlelight . . . That glows each hour of the day . . . And through the longest night . . . It never dims or flickers and . . . It never can go out . . . Because my love for you is one . . . Without the slightest doubt . . . It is a love as boundless as . . . The stars that fill the sky . . . And where is any reason, dear . . . For me to tell you why? . . . You are so wonderful and good . . . So sweet, so kind and true . . . There is not half enough that I . . . Could ever do for you . . . And that is why my love for you . . . Is like a candlelight . . . That makes the day seem brighter and . . . Illuminates the night.

*When you receive the keys to your new home or car, you have
duplicates made, in case of emergency. And when you have lost
your last and only key to something, you turn to the key maker,
whose ingenious methods can replace the missing item without even
removing the lock. That is when you truly appreciate the—*

KEY MAKER

He makes the keys that lock your house . . . And those that fit
your car . . . The ones that keep your strongbox closed . . . And
all the kinds there are . . . He is the guardian of your files . . .
Your suitcase and your trunk . . . The portal to your office and . . .
Your desk with all its junk . . . In older days his tools were all
. . . On which he had to lean . . . Where now his only labor is
. . . To start a small machine . . . Of course he has to check each
key . . . And smooth it off a bit . . . To see that it is perfect and
. . . That it will really fit . . . Yes, he can shape a thousand keys
. . . And yet, however smart . . . He can not ever make the one
. . . That will unlock your heart.

*Remember when the rain came down like a deluge, and the thun-
der and lightning scared you half to death? Maybe it was in your
childhood, or perhaps in grown-up yesterday. But that storm did
come to an end, and the sun appeared, or the night sky grew calm
and clear. Our trials and tribulations are like that. In time—*

THE STORM WILL END

Sometimes when rain and thunder and . . . The blinding lightning blend . . . We have a wild and raging storm . . . That never
seems to end . . . It floods the streets and damages . . . The
houses and the trees . . . And sounds and looks like it would last
. . . For two eternities . . . So are the disappointments that . . .
We meet from day to day . . . The miseries, the tragedies . . . The
tears that come our way . . . Sometimes our troubles multiply . . .
Until our hearts despair . . . And they appear to burden us . . .
Beyond our strength to bear . . . But always by the grace of God
. . . The longest storm will cease . . . And every sad and worried
heart . . . Will find some joy and peace.

*All children like to have the feeling that they "belong." They
yearn to be loved and wanted by others. Our daughter, Kristina, is
no different, and that is why she is always so happy when there is a—*

CALL FOR KRISSIE

The sweetest sound Kristina hears . . . When she is all alone
. . . Is when I call to her and say . . . "You're wanted on the
phone" . . . She may be in her room upstairs . . . Or looking at
TV . . . But when the call is hers, she is . . . As happy as can be
. . . She picks up the receiver and . . . Her voice is loud and
long . . . Beyond my time to listen in . . . Or patience to be strong
. . . But I am always joyful when . . . The message is for her . . .
And there is not another ring . . . I ever would prefer . . . Be-
cause our Krissie loves this life . . . With all her friends and songs
. . . And when they call her on the phone . . . She knows that
she "belongs."

*Wouldn't it be wonderful if all our friends were true friends—
forever true? But some of us, when things go wrong or we get in
trouble, discover that we have only two or three real friends, perhaps
only one. And yet, even one faithful friend is a prized possession,
and who would trade that one for a thousand others? I would treasure him as—*

MY ONE TRUE FRIEND

I thought I had a thousand friends . . . Whatever moon or sun
. . . But when I needed them I found . . . That I had only one
. . . I cherished them, I lived for them . . . I felt that they were
true . . . And then they all deserted me . . . With one exception
—you . . . You are the only one today . . . Who stands beside me
now . . . And cares about the sorrow in . . . The wrinkles on my
brow . . . You are the only one who stayed . . . And did not run
away . . . My one and only faithful friend . . . Forever and a day
. . . God bless you for your faith and love . . . And for your charity . . . You are as much a friend to Him . . . As you have been
to me.

It has been said that there is some selfishness in every form of love. We love someone because it makes us happy, especially if that love is returned. But there are those who love God, wholly from gratitude in their hearts, without expectation of reward. And there are those who love and continue to love another, even though their only return is a cup of bitter rejection or abuse. If only every lover could say truthfully—

I LOVE YOU FOR YOU

I do not love you for myself . . . Or anything I seek . . . I only want your happiness . . . Each day of every week . . . I offer you my heartfelt love . . . For all that you desire . . . And all my strength toward every goal . . . To which you may aspire . . . I hope with all my heart and soul . . . That you will reach your star . . . Where everyone on earth will know . . . How wonderful you are . . . I only wish good luck and health . . . As long as you are living . . . And every blessing great and good . . . That God is always giving . . . I do not love you for myself . . . Or what I want to be . . . Your happiness in life is all . . . That means a thing to me.

If you really believe in God, you have the feeling that He is at your side, and that you can always turn to Him in time of need. As you pray to Him, you say—

YOU ARE MY GOD

Dear God, no matter where I go . . . You seem to be with me . . . In every home, on every street . . . In every memory . . . In health and sickness, smiles and tears . . . In fortune and in loss . . . On every wave that lifts the sea . . . You are my albatross . . . You are the wings on which I soar . . . Above the highest wall . . . And You are all my strength against . . . The greatest waterfall . . . And when I walk in loneliness . . . And bitter is my cup . . . You seem to take me by the hand . . . And gently lift me up . . . You are forever at my side . . . And I can feel You near . . . Believe me, I adore You, God . . . With gratitude sincere.

Today is Lincoln's birthday. Born in a log cabin, struggling up every rung of the ladder, Abraham Lincoln reached the top as a great President, a great patriot, and a great philosopher. His quench-less sense of humor was like a mask that concealed the torment in his heart in time of great decision. As we honor him today, we mourn the climax of his greatness when he became—

THE GREAT MARTYR

Today is Lincoln's birthday and . . . We pause to celebrate . . . The memory of one whose name . . . Will be forever great . . . A man who rose from humbleness . . . To be our President . . . And moved with care and caution but . . . Was never hesitant . . . A foe to all intolerance . . . He struggled day and night . . . For lasting peace and brotherhood . . . In every human right . . . He sorrowed over bloodshed and . . . He wept for those who died . . . And there were few who ever knew . . . How hard he toiled and tried . . . Let us remember him today . . . And all the nation pause . . . To say a prayer for him who was . . . A martyr to his cause.

"Don't put off until tomorrow what you can do today." It is a good saying, but how often do we think of it when a particular task is facing us, much less apply it? We shrug our shoulders, and we fig-ure a little delay won't hurt, and then a little more delay, until it seems hopeless to catch up on our work. Let's make up our mind to—

DO IT TODAY

The work that was so urgent once . . . Is safely put away . . . Now, what are all these other things . . . I ought to do today? . . . Oh, yes, there's this and there is that . . . But they will have to wait . . . I have no minute of the clock . . . To keep another date . . . Tomorrow will be time enough . . . To handle each affair . . . And clear my desk of everything . . . That comes from everywhere . . . But wait a second, let me think . . . What happened yester-day? . . . I tried to shirk my worries and . . . I found it did not pay . . . So let me be more faithful to . . . The duties I must do . . . And tackle each immediately . . . To see my problems through.

St. Valentine's Day is one that has been set aside over the years (without any particular historical significance) as Lovers' Day. We observe it with greeting cards and heart-shaped boxes of candy, and that is nice, but every day we ought to say—

MY VALENTINE

I love you, darling, every day . . . Of every month and year . . . Indeed each golden hour you . . . Become more sweet and dear . . . But when the moment is at hand . . . For valentines and such . . . My feeling of affection has . . . An extra special touch . . . Because I think of all you mean . . . And all that love implies . . . And many more romantic stars . . . Illuminate the skies . . . I see a brighter sun by day . . . A softer moon at night . . . And in your own beloved eyes . . . There is a magic light . . . And so I say this sentiment . . . Forever old and new . . . That I adore you, darling, and . . . I love and treasure you.

Maybe you like to travel by plane or bus. I prefer the train. Of course, if I am in a hurry, I fly—nothing can get you there faster. As for economy—well, you can't beat the bus. But if it fits your budget, if you are not in too big a rush, and if you want a home on wheels, there is nothing like—

GOING BY TRAIN

I board the train to travel to . . . Some city in our nation . . . What is that train to me except . . . A means of transportation? . . . What else is it? I'll tell you what . . . It is my home on wheels . . . Where it is just as comfortable . . . As home-life ever feels . . . And sometimes trains mean even more . . . When I am safe aboard them . . . With all their servants (in my home . . . I never could afford them) . . . The porter and conductor and . . . The one who waits on me . . . At breakfast, lunch or dinner with . . . The utmost courtesy . . . And even to the baggage boy . . . For all his humble station . . . My heart is deeply grateful for . . . Our railroad transportation.

"See a pin, pick it up—all the day you'll have good luck." But where are you going to put that pin when you find it? It is a lucky thing that someone got the idea of a pincushion, a receptacle for pins and needles. More than that, this resting place for sharp points is a chest of family dreams and memories—of little pants and skirts that ran to school, of socks with holes. Love, sacrifice and hope are the stuffing in that old—

PINCUSHION

There is a special cushion for . . . The pins that housewives save . . . To keep our clothes together, from . . . The cradle to the grave . . . The resting place for needles too . . . The tiny and the tall . . . For sewing buttons, darning socks . . . Or anything at all . . . It is the handy article . . . For all the sharpest points . . . That otherwise might penetrate . . . Our feet or other joints . . . It may be new and fancy or . . . A gift from Grandma's day . . . The cushion that preserves the pins . . . That otherwise would stray . . . The cushion for economy . . . To keep us in repair . . . And quietly remind us of . . . A mother's loving care.

An act of kindness is not true charity unless we mean it, and unless we do it voluntarily, without prompting. If we do it be-grudgingly, there is virtually no charity at all. In our benevolence—

WE MUST BE WILLING

No deed of kindness in this life . . . However great it be . . . Is worthy of reward unless . . . We do it willingly . . . It must be truly instant in . . . Response to some request . . . Or something quite spontaneous . . . To please a certain guest . . . If someone asks a favor and . . . We have to hesitate . . . Our charity eventually . . . Is just a little late . . . At home, at work or any place . . . Where one in need may call . . . Unless we act immediately . . . There is no act at all . . . There is no generosity . . . No willingness to give . . . And we deserve no medal for . . . The selfish way we live.

Sursum corda. *When your heart is troubled, when you are weighed down with your worries, and there seems to be no solution to your problems, remember God. "Lift up your hearts," as that Latin phrase exhorts. God loves you, and He is always ready to forgive and to help you. Instead of despairing—*

LOOK UP AND PRAY

If you are troubled in your heart . . . If you are sad today . . . And if the world is cold and bleak . . . Look up to God and pray . . . Tell Him your problems, pour them out . . . Before His mighty throne . . . You will not be the first to plead . . . You will not be alone . . . However futile it may seem . . . How much you may despair . . . There always is the comfort and . . . The peace that comes with prayer . . . If you are not to blame at all . . . He knows that you are true . . . And if you are a sheep that strayed . . . He searches now for you . . . He is as willing to forgive . . . The wrongs that you have done . . . As He is ready to bestow . . . The glory you have won.

What must a man offer a woman when he asks her to become his wife—position, security, wealth? No, not by the marriage vows. There is only one required offer, and that is the promise of faithful love forever on earth. If she loves him, she will accept him, however small his bank account or prospects, as he promises her—

ALL I CAN OFFER

I want to look into your eyes . . . I want to hold your hand . . . I want to whisper in your ear . . . And make you understand . . . I want to draw you close to me . . . And press your lips to mine . . . With every sweet and pleasant taste . . . Of music and of wine . . . And then I must confess to you . . . That I can only bring . . . A humble place in life and just . . . A plain old wedding ring . . . Oh, I would build a palace bright . . . Of silver and of gold . . . With all the gorgeous treasures that . . . Your heart could ever hold . . . But all that I can offer you . . . Of real security . . . Is just my everlasting love . . . And my small salary.

If you are in business, you realize the meaning of an invoice and the importance of paying it on time, whether to take advantage of a discount or merely to keep up your credit rating. You don't like those reminders of your debts any more than your retail customer enjoys his monthly bills, and it sure is a good feeling when you cover that—

INVOICE

An invoice is no silent voice . . . Despite its printed form . . . And when it is not promptly paid . . . It can create a storm . . . An invoice is a statement of . . . The goods dispatched to you . . . The kind and quantity and of . . . The payment that is due . . . It may present a discount good . . . In 10 or 30 days . . . Or else demand the money now . . . In no uncertain phrase . . . An invoice is a memo that . . . Is sent to let you know . . . Your credit will be better if . . . Your payment is not slow . . . It is a piece of paper that . . . Reminds you of your debt . . . But when your check is on its way . . . You have no fear or fret.

The wheels of a bicycle can be the wheels of success. At least they can be the means of propelling a child to school for the education that some day may lead that boy or girl to glory for God, country and home. On rural road or city street, I always think of that when I see a girl or a—

BOY ON A BIKE

A boy rides on his bicycle . . . Along a country lane . . . He likes the sun but does not mind . . . The falling snow or rain . . . The books across his shoulders slung . . . Are on their way to school . . . And he is thinking of this life . . . And of the golden rule . . . He calls hello to Farmer Jones . . . And whistles to a dog . . . And wonders if success could be . . . Like falling off a log . . . If he could be a hero great . . . And make a fortune fast . . . Or he is doomed to labor hard . . . As long as he will last . . . And in his dreams and reveries . . . He pedals on his way . . . To reach the country schoolhouse and . . . To start another day.

The name of George Washington is the symbol of democracy and our United States. The father of our country, our first President, and the soldier who led our forebears to victory over tyranny, will always remain as the greatest American in the hearts of his countrymen. He is—

OUR WASHINGTON

George Washington was truly great . . . And we give thanks today . . . That he began the country that . . . Is now the U.S.A. . . . He led the way to Valley Forge . . . And all throughout the war . . . That we might live in liberty . . . And peace for evermore . . . And ever since he raised the flag . . . To guide his valiant force . . . Our nation has endeavored to . . . Pursue his prudent course . . . He was a mighty statesman and . . . An able president . . . The symbol of democracy . . . And equal government . . . We give our praise to Washington . . . And thank almighty God . . . That one so great belonged to us . . . And walked upon this sod.

When you and your loved one part, and when by some miracle you come together again—whether you disagreed between yourselves, or there were those who interfered—it does not matter now. It is over, and you know in your hearts that there is—

NOTHING TO FORGIVE

You said you would remember me . . . And then you passed me by . . . And though I asked you many times . . . You never told me why . . . You never gave another thought . . . To all our times together . . . Whatever season of the year . . . Or any sort of weather . . . You merely went along your way . . . And did not seem to care . . . If ever I remembered you . . . In any thought or prayer . . . And then you had a change of heart . . . And you were there to meet me . . . With all the love and all the smiles . . . That you could ever greet me . . . And now our lives are joined in love . . . As long as we may live . . . And there is nothing to forget . . . And nothing to forgive.

No day is ever wasted, as long as we arise and mingle with our fellow human beings. Our association and our conversations are bound to teach us something, usually something worth while. It may not make us rich financially but it may inspire us to live a better life. Our every moment with others should help us—

/TO LIVE AND LEARN

If I learn just one little thing . . . This day will be worth while . . . And on the road of progress I . . . Shall pass another mile . . . It may be through experience . . . Or someone's good advice . . . Or some new article I read . . . And think it over twice . . . It need not be a genius or . . . A bit of ancient lore . . . It may be just the wisdom of . . . The guy who lives next door . . . But if I learn and profit in . . . The smallest of amounts . . . I know that I have truly lived . . . Another day that counts . . . If I increase my knowledge in . . . The lowliest of style . . . At least to that extent today . . . My life is more worth while.

Some people are huge, healthy and strong. Some are mentally and politically powerful. A few have all of these attributes combined. Unfortunately, too many who are blest with the gift of supremacy, physical or mental, take the credit unto themselves. They forget that—

ALL THINGS ARE GOD'S

All things in life belong to God . . . The earth, the sky, the sea . . . The atom and the universe . . . And all eternity . . . The man with beard as white as snow . . . The baby born today . . . The ragged little orphan girl . . . Who tries to find her way . . . The gold that fills the guarded grave . . . The silver in a ring . . . And all the joy and sorrow that . . . A smile or tear can bring . . . All things are part of God's design . . . Including you and I . . . And it is not for any soul . . . To ask or wonder why . . . So as our glory may be bright . . . Or keep on getting dim . . . Let us be mindful always that . . . All things belong to Him.

*The honor of being a United States Senator, great as it is, can
never match the responsibility of that position. His voice and his vote
are more powerful in Congress than those of the individual Representative. We hope he is aware of that when he becomes a—*

SENATOR

A senator is one who helps . . . Our government to live . . .
With somewhat more importance than . . . A representative . . .
He usually is well informed . . . On all the turns and tricks . . .
To handle legislation in . . . The best of politics . . . And he has
greater power with . . . His solitary voice . . . Than many other
officers . . . Who are the people's choice . . . Of course he may
be wrong at times . . . And make a sad mistake . . . But he is
there to do his best . . . For everybody's sake . . . And if he really
wants to keep . . . His office on the hill . . . He does his best to
serve his state . . . And do his people's will.

*Day after day we give our thoughts to our relatives and our friends,
to mere acquaintances, and sometimes even to mere strangers on the
street. These thoughts are occasional, as a rule. Now and then they
are frequent. But our constant thoughts are for the one we love the
most. No other thoughts could come—*

SO OFTEN

How often do I think of you . . . When we must be apart? . . .
As often as I have to breathe . . . To keep alive my heart . . . As
often as I walk on earth . . . And there are skies above . . . And
just as often as my lips . . . May utter words of love . . . There is
no intermission, dear . . . There is no time to pause . . . And all
the thoughts I have of you . . . Are free from any flaws . . . They
are my loving thoughts of you . . . Each moment of each day . . .
And when the purple of the night . . . Has put the sun away . . .
I think of you so often and . . . How much you mean to me . . .
I may as well confess, my dear . . . I love you constantly.

t the American view, one of the greatest luxuries is a new car.
hether we can afford one each year or only once in five or ten
years, that shiny, modern form of transportation is a real thrill. And,
oh, the interior smells so good! That is how my family and I felt
when we got—

OUR NEW CAR

At last my wife agreed with me . . . To buy a modern car . . .
A shiny, speedy model for . . . Our travels near and far . . . And
so we turned the old one in . . . Though not without regret . . .
For there were many pleasant miles . . . We never shall forget
. . . But now we have a brand new car . . . And, oh, it smells so
good . . . And everyone admires it . . . Around our neighbor-
hood . . . And now my family and I . . . Can hardly wait to start
. . . The happy travels we have mapped . . . In our vacation heart
. . . It is a bracing tonic that . . . Is filled with magic cheer . . .
I only wish we could afford . . . A new car every year.

Whoever originated leap year had a wonderful idea. Although
there is nothing amiss in a lady's proposing marriage, it is tradition
that the man should bend his knee to her. Thanks to someone, eve
fourth year has become—

HER TIME TO LEAP

One year in four the lady is . . . Allowed to take a lea
And grab that bashful gentleman . . . She wants to claim a
. . . In all the best propriety . . . She may propose to
And swear that she will satisfy . . . His every wish and w
Of course he may not fall for it . . . And then again he
But she must take the chance that she . . . Can bring
bay . . . It is her opportunity . . . To make her feel
. . . Without resorting to her wiles . . . Her smile
. . . And when the words are spoken and . . . His li
kissed . . . The gentleman is usually . . . Too feebl

Privacy can be a cold aloneness, as when you close the door to your private office. But privacy can be warm and peaceful, both inside and out—especially at home—and you can be alone without feeling alone. All you need are some inviting—

CURTAINS AND DRAPES

I like the curtains and the drapes . . . That decorate each room
. . . To make a pretty picture and . . . To chase away the gloom
. . . I like the fluffy curtains as . . . They billow in the breeze
. . . And when there is no wind and they . . . Are quiet as you
please . . . The stately drapes that kiss the floor . . . With calm
and dignity . . . And seem to open and to close . . . Each soulful
memory . . . They give me privacy when I . . . Retire or arise
. . . They are the handy little lids . . . That shut my neighbor's
eyes . . . The curtains and the drapes that seem . . . To dissipate
the gloom . . . And lend their warmth and beauty to . . . The
walls of every room.

Each new friend is another investment of our faith in life and in our fellow man. If our new friend turns out to be a true friend, our investment will pay rich dividends in happiness; otherwise, we may have to write off a loss. As for me, each friend becomes a permanent deposit to, or a sudden withdrawal from—

MY FRIENDSHIP BANK

I keep my richest savings in . . . A special bank account . . .
And every time the balance jumps . . . My happy spirits mount
. . . Because each new deposit is . . . A friend that I have found
. . . And therefore my investment is . . . A project safe and sound
. . . I have my friendship passbook with . . . Each entry old and
new . . . And interest is recorded as . . . They grow more dear and
true . . . I never make withdrawals if . . . It can be helped at all
. . . But if I have to make one, it . . . Is always very small . . .
Not anything compared to that . . . Original amount . . . Of some
misjudged deposit to . . . My friendship bank account.

Sometimes it seems that married couples who do not want children, have them, while those who yearn for them are denied this miracle of life. Fortunately, marriages blest with babies are the great majority. But here and there some husband and wife must turn to God and pray—

GIVE US A CHILD

Give us, O God, one child to love . . . A baby girl or boy . . . Please bless our marriage union with . . . This miracle of joy . . . An infant that will live and grow . . . To normal weight and height . . . And through its earthly years become . . . More worthy in Your sight . . . A man or woman in this world . . . To spread Your gospel true . . . By everything that he or she . . . May undertake to do . . . We promise You, Almighty God . . . That we will strive each day . . . To teach our child to praise Your name . . . And follow in Your way . . . Give us the blessing of a child . . . That we may do our part . . . To carry on creation with . . . Another human heart.

Unfortunately, love is not like law. If the object of your affection doubts the sincerity of your sentiments, there is little or nothing that you can do to prove it. The only proof of true love is faith, and that proof remains final unless and until the faith is destroyed. As you have faith in your loved one, so your loved one should have faith in you. And so all you can do is hope and lastly say—

BUT IF YOU DOUBT

Why do you not believe in me? . . . Why is it that you doubt? . . . What is there in my life, my love . . . You want to know about? . . . My life is all an open book . . . For you to read each page . . . However small or tall I was . . . Whatever was my age . . . Go through the book, investigate . . . Each page of it is true . . . The only words of love I spoke . . . Were those I said to you . . . You are the only one on earth . . . Who ever held my heart . . . And only you could comfort it . . . Or tear it all apart . . . But if you still are doubtful, dear . . . One moment of today . . . I shall be grateful for your smile . . . And I will go away.

Maybe you don't like to get up in public and sing and cheer and backslap. Maybe you are shy about advertising your name and product—but, brother, if you are an American, and if you believe in companionship, free enterprise, and civic and community welfare, you ought to join a—

SERVICE CLUB

The service club is one that meets . . . For luncheon every week
. . . To sing and eat, review reports . . . And hear some person speak . . . It is the best of fellowship . . . In true commercial style . . . And in a lot of other ways . . . It makes itself worth while . . . It sponsors education and . . . The many projects free
. . . That are of vital interest to . . . The whole community . . . The children and their welfare, the . . . Utilities in town . . . And how to keep the progress up . . . And hold the taxes down
. . . It is the organization where . . . The common elbows rub
. . . God bless the growing membership . . . Of every service club.

You send birthday cards to your relatives and friends, and you receive greetings on your own birthday. But do you know why those messages of love and friendship are exchanged? Has it ever occurred to you? It is because someone is glad that someone else was born—a special someone—who now has another—

BIRTHDAY *Jack*

A birthday is a special time . . . For every girl and boy . . . With greeting cards and presents and . . . A party filled with joy
. . . A birthday is a certain date . . . Young men and maids prefer
. . . When she remembers him, or he . . . Bestows a gift on her
. . . And when the wedding bells have rung . . . A birthday means much more . . . If only in the necktie new . . . Or flowers at the door . . . But as the years go slipping by . . . Her birthday slips his mind . . . While he is hoping that his own . . . No calendar will find . . . But birthdays have a curious way . . . Of coming every year . . . So why not take them as they come . . . And face them with good cheer?

Our dictionaries still include the word, "hændkerchief," although today—with tissues for the nose and hands—it has dwindled to the romantic "kerchief" for the gentleman's breast pocket or milady's gown. Dwindled? Well, in length of name only. Actually it has grown, in dignity, as the unused, sanitary and decorative—

MODERN KERCHIEF

The kerchief used to be a cloth . . . That tended to the nose . . . Where now it is an article . . . That helps to strike a pose . . . The gentleman protrudes it from . . . A pocket on his breast . . . To match the color of his tie . . . So he may look his best . . . The lady has more use for it . . . She pins it on her dress . . . Or uses it to dab the tears . . . Of hurt or happiness . . . She drops it deftly on the floor . . . At some romantic time . . . Or she forgets it at the scene . . . Where there has been a crime . . . The kerchief has become a part . . . Of putting on a pose . . . While there are paper tissues now . . . For servicing the nose.

Do you believe in love at first sight—or second, or third? Maybe it took you a long while to realize that you were in love, but more than likely you were in love from the very beginning. Think back to that first meeting, and you will probably tell yourself: That was why—

I LINGERED

It was not just your manner or . . . That magic of your smile . . . That prompted me to look at you . . . And linger for a while . . . But there was something quite profound . . . That made my feelings stir . . . It seemed as though I saw the soul . . . That shaped your character . . . A character of goodness and . . . Of all the virtues bright . . . That lift the dawn and dissipate . . . The shadows of the night . . . And so I lingered for a while . . . And when we met again . . . My view of you was just as true . . . As ever it was then . . . And now I know with all my heart . . . Whatever moon or sun . . . My love is yours forever and . . . You are my only one.

Our pencil and typewriter erasers come in handy. They r̲
many an error. Of course they cannot wash away all our mistakes ̲ ̲.
often they help us change our thoughts and set things right, and we
are grateful for any and all—

ERASURES

Erasures are the arrows strong . . . That hit their target true . . .
To splinter and destroy mistakes . . . That could be charged to you
. . . They are the ones that people make . . . Before they give a
speech . . . And help professors on their way . . . Each time they
start to teach . . . For there is no erasure that . . . Is ever thought
or made . . . Unless you honestly believe . . . It will improve
your grade . . . No one can sing a perfect song . . . The first time
that he tries . . . Or write a poem that will last . . . As long as all
the skies . . . There have to be erasures through . . . Our struggle
and our strife . . . Because we know from our mistakes . . . There
is no perfect life.

March 10

Are you healthy and strong? What makes you so? Do you exercise
every day? Do you feel that you are building up your body to the
best of your ability? Is your body something within your power to
make or break, or do you ever think of God and tell Him humbly—

THANK YOU FOR HEALTH

I thank You, God, for giving me . . . The health I have today
. . . With mind and heart and body and . . . The hands to make
my way . . . I know I am no creature strong . . . With sinews
made of steel . . . And sometimes I complain about . . . The
feebleness I feel . . . But I still have the moral strength . . . The
courage and the will . . . To serve You faithfully, my God . . .
And all my vows fulfill . . . So may it be as long as blood . . . Is
flowing through my veins . . . With credit and with gratitude
. . . To You for all my gains . . . And so I bow before Your throne
. . . And say this fervent prayer . . . That You will always keep
my health . . . In Your beloved care.

We may build the finest, most expensive house in the world, and yet it may never be a home. What makes a home? Four walls can make a home but not by their physical durability or the richness of their décor. They must be the walls that surround a warm family life. The love of spouse for spouse, the laughter of children, and now and then the tears—these make the home within—

FOUR WALLS

A home may have a dozen rooms . . . Or it may have just one . . . It all depends upon the walls . . . That glisten in the sun . . . Of course there must be four but they . . . Must be a special kind . . . To make a house become a home . . . With happiness of mind . . . There has to be a wall of faith . . . A wall of unity . . . A wall of hope, and one of love . . . For all the family . . . These are the four and only walls . . . That weather every storm . . . Around a peaceful fireplace . . . That keeps affection warm . . . Within these walls the soul will grow . . . The weary body rest . . . Where friends will call, and God will be . . . The everlasting Guest.

No poem, no letter of love, or any other flowery expression can improve on those words, "I love you." Just three little words, they are clear as a bell and, more than any other, they have the ring of sincerity. When I whisper them to my beloved, they are—

MY WORDS SINCERE

How many ways are there in all . . . To say I love you, dear? . . . How many ways to whisper love . . . Apparently sincere? . . . Perhaps in Spanish or in French . . . Or other Romance tongue . . . Some phrases sound more beautiful . . . When they are said or sung . . . Or possibly in poetry . . . There is a certain rhyme . . . That seems to hold the fragrance of . . . The flowers of all time . . . But all of them mean nothing if . . . The heart is not sincere . . . And so I choose these simple words . . . To say I love you, dear . . . Because when I am with you or . . . We have to be apart . . . I mean each syllable and I . . . Am speaking to your heart.

If only God had made the human being without a temper! Just imagine how peaceful life on earth would be. There would never be a war or a fight of any kind. Even a mere difference of opinion could not cause the slightest trouble. But we have that temper, and we get mad, sometimes too easily. More than often the fault is our own. Think it over, and the next time you start to boil over, why not just—

GET MAD AT YOU

If you must have an angry mood . . . As people sometimes do . . . Then go ahead and get real mad . . . But take it out on you . . . Just go away and hide yourself . . . With every jibe and taunt . . . And let your temperature go up . . . To any height you want . . . You may have been the righteous one . . . And someone did you wrong . . . But in the flame of fury you . . . Will never get along . . . And it is barely possible . . . That it has been your fault . . . And with a bit of compromise . . . You might have called a halt . . . So keep your anger to yourself . . . And strive to arbitrate . . . And you will hold your honored place . . . Among the truly great.

You seldom see him, you are hardly aware of him, and yet he risks his life in time of emergency to save the lives of others, perhaps your own. He has a humble but important job. He is your—

TELEPHONE LINEMAN

He puts the pole into the ground . . . And then he climbs up there . . . To string the lines so voices may . . . Be carried everywhere . . . And when repairs are needed, he . . . Is there to mend each thread . . . As when a hunter aims at birds . . . And hits the lines instead . . . But, more importantly, he meets . . . Those great emergencies . . . When fire, flood and blinding storm . . . Create their tragedies . . . He risks his life that we may send . . . Our frantic SOS . . . Whenever our community . . . Is stricken with distress . . . Indeed he is a hero as . . . He labors high above . . . For business, home and government . . . And all who are in love.

When the time is at hand to pay income tax, some people worry or complain. The best philosophy I know on this score is what a man told me once. "Income tax," he said, "doesn't worry me, as long as I can pay it. If the day comes when I can't pay it, then I'll start to worry." As for those who complain, they should stop and think of what would happen to our country, our government, and our way of living, if we did not all do—

OUR SHARE TODAY

It may be quite a task today . . . To pay our income tax . . . And maybe we resent the law . . . But let us face the facts . . . The freedom of our U.S.A. . . . And our security . . . Depend upon a government . . . Of true democracy . . . A government in which we all . . . Agree to do our share . . . According to our common thought . . . Of what is just and fair . . . And as our nation's problems and . . . Our pocketbooks expand . . . So we must be prepared to meet . . . Our government's demand . . . And how would any war be waged . . . That we might ever win . . . Except as every one of us . . . Were willing to chip in?

Happiness is built on friendship and good will to our fellow man. Why not wish our neighbor well? A wish is a word. It does not cost anything. Even if our heart is not quite in it, God will bless us for saying to someone—

WISHING YOU WELL

There is no warmer feeling or . . . A more enchanting spell . . . Than just to hear some person say . . . The words that wish you well . . . The kindly greeting from a friend . . . Who gives his hand to you . . . Or from a stranger in the town . . . That you are passing through . . . "The best of luck," "A pleasant trip" . . . "God speed you on your way" . . . And all the good expressions that . . . Invite a brighter day . . . It is a little thing in life . . . That means so very much . . . If only in the spirit of . . . Its gentle, human touch . . . There might be less of sorrow and . . . Of tragedy to tell . . . If everyone sincerely smiled . . . And wished each other well.

The Irish and St. Patrick's Day have become so much a part of American tradition, it is a wonder that we have not become the United States of America and Ireland. It seems that no other nationality has blended in so well with all that stands for democracy, and no other sons of a foreign sod are such an enormous part of our governmental and community life. God bless them all—that's why—

WE LOVE THE IRISH

If we should count the Irishmen . . . Throughout the U.S.A. . . . They would outnumber those who live . . . In Ireland today . . . The firemen, policemen or . . . Whatever be their call . . . And all the politicians who . . . Invade the city hall . . . O'Toole and Duffey, Shanahan . . . O'Brien and O'Rourke . . . From Murphysboro, Illinois . . . To Yuma and New York . . . We're proud of all the Irish and . . . Their wearin' o' the green . . . Particularly every pert . . . And beautiful colleen . . . God bless their contribution to . . . Our mighty U.S.A. . . . Especially and lovingly . . . On this St. Patrick's Day.

There are all kinds of bells in this world—doorbells, sleigh bells, fire bells, and those that sound the alarm clock or telephone—but the sweetest and most peaceful sound of all is when we hear the pealing of the—

CHURCH BELLS

When church bells ring on Sunday morn . . . I never feel alone . . . Because they have a friendly and . . . A most inviting tone . . . And as I listen to their chimes . . . I seem to hear them say . . . Their silvery sounds are calling me . . . To worship God today . . . Their music is a melody . . . That fills the heart and soul . . . And summons all the sinners to . . . Attain their golden goal . . . The church bells sing celestial songs . . . With echoes soft and clear . . . And there is something sanctified . . . About the atmosphere . . . I feel the presence of my God . . . As I go on my way . . . To visit Him and worship Him . . . Inside the church today.

Did you have a busy day at the office, factory, restaurant, hotel, or wherever you work? If you did, then surely the time seemed to fly. But if you were somewhat idle most of the day, the clock moved slowly. That is the common measurement of—

OUR WORKING DAY

The working day is just as long . . . As we decide to make it . . . According to our will to toil . . . Or if we try to shake it . . . The moments will be fleeting and . . . The hours will go faster . . . If we resist the urge to loaf . . . And strive to be the master . . . But if we simply sit around . . . And sort of take it easy . . . The time will drag and we will find . . . The day is never breezy . . . There is no slow and lazy way . . . To climb the working ladder . . . And wastefulness will only make . . . The boss a little madder . . . So let us do our best and most . . . And be a busy beaver . . . And soon the time will fly and we . . . Will catch the working fever.

If your bride-to-be doesn't know much about cooking, and if she is somewhat unfamiliar with housework, just tell her that you will be glad to help her out all you can. There will be time for her to learn these things, as well as time to learn that your generous offer was a loving subterfuge. Yes—

THERE WILL BE TIME

I do not love you for myself . . . Or what I want to do . . . There simply is no other one . . . As wonderful as you . . . I love you for yourself, my sweet . . . With all the heart in me . . . And wish you all the happiness . . . That there could ever be . . . I want to be of service, dear . . . In every way I can . . . And that includes the mop and broom . . . And every frying pan . . . Yes, I will help you keep our house . . . Our lawn and flower-beds . . . And I will kiss your lips each time . . . The pansies raise their heads . . . Of course, my dear, I do expect . . . A little in return . . . But after we are wed, there will . . . Be time for you to learn.

When God made the world He also created nature. He fashioned the nature that turns day into night, winter to spring, sunshine to rain, and rain into snow. Very likely He did this to give life variety, to keep up our interest and enthusiasm, or even the curiosity that some of us need in order to go on living. And so, as the seasons begin their cycle again, let us—

THANK GOD FOR SPRING

God made the winter and the spring . . . The summer and the fall . . . And only by His loving grace . . . Is anything at all . . . The human heart, immortal soul . . . Each baby that is born . . . The twilight with its silver stars . . . The glory of each morn . . . Each mineral and vegetable . . . And animal on earth . . . Is God's creation in this life . . . However small its worth . . . And so as we enjoy this world . . . And spring is at our door . . . Let us recall His blessings and . . . Give thanks to Him once more . . . Our thanks for every shower and . . . Each flower from the ground . . . And every inspiration in . . . The beauty all around.

Some people are born to be wise in the ways of business. Such was never my fortune, and today I would surely be an easy mark for any sharp tradesman, except for one thing—the fact that I married the right girl. Expertly she guides me in—

MY BUSINESS DEALS

In my important business deals . . . Some people think of me . . . As being just as ignorant . . . As anyone can be . . . And they are not exactly wrong . . . Because the truth reveals . . . That I know very little when . . . It comes to business deals . . . But they are wrong in thinking they . . . Can make a profit fast . . . For there is my good wife with whom . . . They must contend at last . . . They may not ever see her face . . . Or hear her charming voice . . . But she is there to counsel me . . . And help me make my choice . . . And if there ever was a wife . . . And business woman smart . . . It is the lovely lady who . . . Is dearest to my heart.

Why do we poke our nose into other people's business? Haven't we problems and troubles enough of our own? When will we ever learn to "live and let live"? Everyone has the right to live his own life. There should be—

NO INTERFERENCE

Each person has his life to live . . . His task to move a stone . . . Why does he not go on and leave . . . Another to his own? . . . Why must he try to interfere . . . With someone else's way . . . And dictate unto others how . . . To use the night and day? . . . He merely is a mortal and . . . He has no moral right . . . To set up human standards and . . . Propose their daily plight . . . Dictators, kings and emperors . . . Have tried without success . . . And only those who worshiped God . . . Have found their happiness . . . So let no person interfere . . . But each one live today . . . In freedom and in brotherhood . . . According to God's way.

Some girls may like it but others find it disheartening to be tossed into a stenographic pool, where they must take dictation from any of a dozen men. They are faced with the problem of constantly trying to adjust themselves to different voices, temperaments, etc. Of course, one of those voices may speak for a good marriage prospect and a way out of the—

STENO POOL

The stenographic pool is one . . . In which the ladies swim . . . Who have to take dictation from . . . A different kind of "him" . . . They never know if he will be . . . The sweet or surly kind . . . With business or designing thoughts . . . Or nothing on his mind . . . He may be handsome and adroit . . . Or just another guy . . . Without appeal of any sort . . . To make a spinster sigh . . . And so it goes from day to day . . . The stenographic pool . . . That may promote stenographers . . . Or flunk them out of "school" . . . But they have opportunities . . . To make their special choice . . . And now and then their heart is set . . . Upon a special voice.

"Thou shalt love thy neighbor as thyself." That is not always an easy thing to do, and there are those neighbors who try our patience. But that is God's commandment, and He will reward us richly for any charity we extend in thought, word or deed. At least we can pray and say to God: Please, help me now—

) LOVE MY NEIGHBOR

not for myself . . . (Though I need many prayers)
brothers burdened now . . . With more important
w I have my troubles, God . . . And they are not
others may have bigger ones . . . They want to
. I pray that You will hear them first . . . And let
. . Although it may turn out their faults . . . Are
mine . . . I want to help my neighbor, God . . .
ll each day . . . In everything I do and think . . .
I say . . . I pray that You will put their sins . . .
en shelf . . . And help me love my neighbor more
uld love myself.

A woman in India stood by a temple in process of construction. A missionary asked her the cost of the building. She looked at the questioner in surprise and answered, "Why, we do not know. It is for our god. We don't count the cost."—
Mississippi Nazarene,

The WORD and WAY

a beautiful word. It denotes a person in love and espoused to another *"until death do us part." It is (or should be) like a song of eternal devotion. But so often, as time goes by, we grow careless and indifferent, and we take each other for granted. In moments of disagreement we are inclined to say, "After all, I AM your husband (or wife)," when we should be remembering and saying—*

I AM YOUR SPOUSE

I am your spouse in every way . . . That I could ever be . . . To live and serve you any time . . . Your heart may call to me . . . I am your own to comfort you . . . To help and understand . . . If just to smile into your eyes . . . And hold your trembling hand . . . Whatever worries you may have . . . Of deeds or phrases said . . . I will not argue, criticize . . . Or ever leave your bed . . . I am your own to have and hold . . . As much as you are mine . . . And only for your happiness . . . Have I the least design . . . I am your spouse in every way . . . I promised God and you . . . And by His grace and with your help . . . I shall be ever true.

[51]

Few policemen ever really retire. Most take a job as a guard or special watchman, either to keep active and pass away time, or to supplement their retirement income. Whatever his motive, we have a warm place in our heart for the one who turns to supervising our school patrol—the one who becomes the guardian angel in traffic for our boys and girls. We love that—

OLD POLICEMAN

The old policeman never dies . . . Nor does he fade away . . . As those retired soldiers who . . . Have seen a better day . . . He is the keen and private eye . . . In some important bank . . . Or in another enterprise . . . He holds an equal rank . . . His job is plant protection or . . . He watches personnel . . . To check on workers' loyalty . . . And see that all is well . . . But most of all we love the one . . . Who fills the daily role . . . Of supervising traffic with . . . The youthful school patrol . . . Who helps to guide the boys and girls . . . When classes end or start . . . He never dies or fades away . . . But lingers in our heart.

When I go to bed I want to sleep and have pleasant dreams. I prefer not to have a nightmare, even though it is said to be an indication of sound and peaceful slumber. Just let me sleep. You can keep your—

NIGHTMARE

They say a nightmare is a sign . . . Of sound and restful sleep . . . But where my slumber is concerned . . . Their nightmares they can keep . . . I dream of getting off a train . . . In sleepy-time array . . . And rushing back in time to see . . . My Pullman pull away . . . I dream of elevators that . . . Begin to drop and drop . . . And keep on whizzing down and down . . . With never any stop . . . Or else someone is chasing me . . . With pistol or a knife . . . And I have not the strength to run . . . Not even for my life . . . A nightmare may be good to have . . . But more and more I doubt it . . . It always makes me scared to death . . . I'd rather sleep without it.

Success is not around the corner. It does not grow on trees. It takes time to find it—lots of time—because you have to earn it. Of course, you may be a genius, an exception to the rule, but for the average person there is—

NO SUDDEN GLORY

Some people always run along . . . The roadway to success . . . When they should walk with easy stride . . . In search of happiness . . . They strive to reach their goal today . . . Or, at the least, tomorrow . . . Until their disillusionment . . . Becomes a world of sorrow . . . Success is not a sudden thing . . . That comes in early years . . . But usually it takes its time . . . With many smiles and tears . . . Of course there are those certain ones . . . More talented or clever . . . Who seem to strike it lucky in . . . Their very first endeavor . . . But most success is slow and hard . . . It is not overnight . . . It stems from faith and patience and . . . The persevering fight.

Flowers are fair and lovely when they come from your own garden, and you treasure them in your home because you planted and nursed them. But what about the flowers that knock on your door or ring your bell—the gift from a friend or relative? Don't they smell just a little sweeter? Isn't there a little extra fragrance? It seems that way to me when I put them in—

MY FLOWER VASE

I love the pretty flowers in . . . Their sunny garden-place . . . But even more I love the ones . . . Inside a special vase . . . The beautiful receptacle . . . That someone sent to me . . . With blossoms for a birthday or . . . Our anniversary . . . It is a vessel filled with love . . . Whatever size or shade . . . That keeps the fragrant memories . . . Of all the blooms that fade . . . I never leave it empty for . . . The fraction of a day . . . For if no flowers come from friends . . . I make my own bouquet . . . But everywhere around the house . . . I treasure each new vase . . . Each one to me a memory . . . Of some familiar face.

You are in love, and you want your loved one to know it. But your time is taken up when you are apart. Perhaps you are the husband, busy at the office, or you are the wife, running around in circles, trying to keep house, do the shopping, etc. Still, your thoughts can be together, as you say—

ALL I CAN SPARE

I have a busy schedule, dear . . . With many things to do . . . But when I have some time to spare . . . I always think of you . . . Each moment and each hour that . . . I have for rest or play . . . I dedicate to thoughts of you . . . Whatever night or day . . . And there are those occasions when . . . You interrupt my schemes . . . As surely as your smiling face . . . Is always in my dreams . . . You are the dawn that wakes me and . . . The sand that fills my eyes . . . When stars are whispering good night . . . Among the sleepy skies . . . To you belongs each second of . . . Each minute I can spare . . . Because you are the only one . . . For whom I really care.

April Fool's Day is a time for jokes and fun—but only the sensible kind. All kinds of tricks are in order if they do not hurt anyone. Let's all enjoy April Fool's Day but not—

APRIL FOOLISHNESS

The foolishness of April Fool . . . Is evident today . . . In all the mean and dirty tricks . . . Some people try to play . . . It is the time to have some fun . . . And get a laugh or two . . . With something to astonish or . . . Perhaps embarrass you . . . But there must be a limit to . . . The tricks on you and me . . . Especially the kind that can . . . Become a tragedy . . . Let us be sensible today . . . And not mix fun with fear . . . By being cruel or unkind . . . Or causing any tear . . . Let's have our April Fool but not . . . Perform the foolish part . . . That causes someone injury . . . Or hurts the human heart.

God knows my thoughts, and He knows my prayers. Even whe *ask special favors for myself, He knows that I am really asking th* *for my family. Whatever blessings He bestows on me, I pass them* *on to my loved ones. He knows I love them, and that they are the* *only ones who matter, the only ones of whom I think—*

WHENEVER I PRAY

Whenever I implore my God . . . To bless and comfort me . . . I really have in mind His grace . . . For my dear family . . . I want His blessing for my spouse . . . And for our hearth and home . . . And for our children good and true . . . Wherever they may roam . . . I pray to God for all the help . . . He is disposed to give . . . But only for my dear ones as . . . Their representative . . . I want them to enjoy this life . . . And all its beauties share . . . And be with God each hour and . . . Forever in His care . . . My every prayer to God is meant . . . For my dear family . . . And after He has blest their hearts . . . May He remember me.

April 3

Turn back the calendar of this book to early January—to the *eighth day, to be exact. The year is like a day, and as the month of* *April is here, this day is drawing nigh to noon. Are you ahead or* *behind, or just about even? The clock keeps ticking. The sun is* *rising higher. It is the—*

YEAR'S LATE MORN

The year is like a single day . . . That fades away so soon . . . And when the month of April starts . . . That day is nearing noon . . . How much are we accomplishing . . . This morning of the year? . . . How is our courage holding up? . . . Our faith to conquer fear? . . . Are we still striving to fulfill . . . Each pledge and noble scheme . . . Or have our resolutions lost . . . Their polish and their gleam? . . . The dawn is gone, the clock ticks on . . . The sun is climbing high . . . Our golden opportunities . . . Are swiftly passing by . . . If we have fallen, let us rise . . . And turn to God once more . . . With fervent prayer to climb each stair . . . And make a higher score.

*When we travel along the highway, we often wonder where to
stop and eat. There are all sorts of cafés, restaurants and lunchrooms.
Some are expensive, some are not. Some have good food, others don't.
The costly dining rooms are easy to spot, but if we are trying to
economize, and if we want plain, wholesome food, then let's keep
on driving until we see that familiar sign—*

TRUCK STOP

When hunger hits you on the road . . . And you would like a
treat . . . Look not for special places where . . . The fancy people
eat . . . Of course there are the restaurants . . . Hotels and quaint
cafés . . . With all the dishes they prepare . . . In their expensive
ways . . . But if you like economy . . . And food that is the best
. . . Then stop your car beside the joint . . . Where heavy haulers
rest . . . Those truckers know their way around . . . Alone or in
a bunch . . . To have their breakfast, dinner or . . . To take a bite
of lunch . . . Be on the lookout for the place . . . Where "TRUCK
STOP" is the sign . . . And if you see some customers . . . It is
the place to dine.

*There are some things in life that we can love without actually
wanting them. We are content to admire them. But as for loving the
opposite sex—and being really in love—we cannot say in truth, "I
love you," unless we also say and really mean—*

I WANT YOU

You ask me if I want you, dear . . . What phrases can I say . .
To tell your loving heart how much . . . You mean to me today?
. . . I want you more than I have loved . . . A doll or teddy-bear
. . . And all the toys and grown-up joys . . . That anyone could
share . . . I want you with my heart and soul . . . With trust and
sympathy . . . And all that I could offer you . . . If you belonged
to me . . . You mean much more to me than all . . . The trophies
on my shelf . . . Or any other glories I . . . Could gather to myself
I want you more, my dearest one . . . Than you will ever know
. . . Because you are so charming and . . . Because I love you so.

*Friendship ought to be on an equal basis, where each tries to help
the other. There is nothing wrong in wanting to get ahead of your
friend when it comes to doing favors. It is a noble motive, but your
friend probably has the same idea, and it might be better if each of
you took your—*

FRIENDSHIP'S TURN

I want to be your dearest friend . . . As much as I can be . . .
Because you have been kind enough . . . To be a friend to me . . .
Because your friendship happily . . . Has given me a debt . . . Of
everlasting gratitude . . . That I will not forget . . . I want to pay
you back in full . . . And then a little more . . . Until, if possible,
I hold . . . The long end of the score . . . And so it will become
your turn . . . To be a friend, and then . . . When you have done
your favor, it . . . Will be my turn again . . . And thus our friendship will go on . . . With every kind endeavor . . . And you and
I will be good friends . . . Forever and forever.

*On those rare occasions when I have to substitute for my wife as
cook, I envy her. I wish I could prepare each meal for the children.
I claim no culinary ability, but the smiles and thanks on the youngsters' lips when they have filled their tummies make me wish they
owed their every meal to me. That's why I love—*

TO COOK FOR THEM

I know how hard all mothers work . . . (God bless my sweetheart's soul) . . . But sometimes I am envious . . . Of every
mother's role . . . And that is when my wife is ill . . . Or she has
gone away . . . And I must keep the children on . . . Their schedule for the day . . . Prepare their breakfast, pack their lunch . . .
And see them off to school . . . And try to cook a dinner that . . .
Will really make them drool . . . Of course I know the thousand
tasks . . . A mother has to face . . . And by the stove or anywhere
. . . I could not fill her place . . . But, oh, I envy her the chance
. . . To keep their bodies fed . . . And kiss their happy tummies
when . . . She tucks them into bed.

About this time of year the Christian world commemorates Good Friday. That was the day Jesus Christ carried His cross to Calvary, was crucified, died, and was buried. He died to redeem humanity from the sins that nailed Him to the cross, including all sins to this day, even as now we make Him suffer. For our salvation—

THIS DAY HE DIED

This day the world commemorates . . . The cross on Calvary . . . Where Jesus Christ was crucified . . . And died for you and me . . . He suffered there for all the sins . . . That weigh our souls today . . . That mankind might remember Him . . . And live a better way . . . He died for us that we might live . . . Beyond this earthly life . . . And in His glory rise above . . . Our hatreds and our strife . . . Then let us kneel and pray today . . . In sorrow deep and true . . . And with repentance for our wrongs . . . Let us begin anew . . . Let us be faithful unto God . . . And grateful to His Son . . . For all the agony that He . . . Endured for everyone.

As you go through life you can never quite appreciate events as they take place, especially as they concern you. Later on, you forget all the heartaches and sorrows, and you think only of the happy times you had. You sort of long for the past, as you are—

LOOKING BACK

When we review our memories . . . And live our lives again . . . Some happenings seem funny that . . . Were not so funny then . . . Some things appear quite thrilling now . . . In quiet memory . . . But at that time they could have spelled . . . A cruel tragedy . . . The labor looks less wearisome . . . And every joy more real . . . Than in the days when eyes beheld . . . And hearts were there to feel . . . And so as we grow older and . . . Our backward vision less . . . We minimize old sorrow and . . . Inflate the happiness . . . And also age informs us that . . . When we were young and new . . . We could not quite appreciate . . . What we were going through.

The sun never shone so brightly, the air was never so sweet, and fear in the hearts of evil men was never so great as on this day in history. It was the day of the Resurrection, when Jesus Christ rose from His grave to open the gates of Heaven for the salvation of souls. Let us praise The Lord, our God. Let us rejoice and sing—

HOSANNA

The Roman guards are sleeping and . . . The stone is rolled away . . . The Lord has risen from His grave . . . It is our Easter Day . . . Hosanna to The Highest and . . . All glory be to God . . . Who gave His only Son to be . . . Our Saviour on this sod . . . The Baby Jesus Whom He sent . . . Was truly Christ The King . . . And we are grateful for His love . . . And all His suffering . . . With all our hearts we do believe . . . And kneel before His throne . . . To worship Him and pray that all . . . Our sins we may atone . . . And as this Easter morning is . . . A holy memory . . . Let us remember Him with love . . . Who died on Calvary.

Perhaps more than any other part of this season, April is typical of spring. We associate this month with rain, the freshness of earth, the budding promise of flowers, and the first call to outdoor life. Lord Tennyson must have been thinking of April when he wrote, "In the spring a young man's fancy," for surely the world is filled with love—

WHEN APRIL COMES

I love the rains of April and . . . The flowers in the spring . . . I love the grasses that are green . . . And all the birds that sing . . . The baseball and the tennis ball . . . The marbles on the ground . . . The babies in their carriages . . . And laughter all around . . . I smell the sweetness in the air . . . I drink the dew of dawn . . . And dreams are happy in my sleep . . . When all the world is gone . . . I love the days of April and . . . Its nights of silver stars . . . And those of drizzles and of fogs . . . That shroud the passing cars . . . I love the month of April with . . . Its blessings from above . . . But most of all when April comes . . . I love the one I love.

Most school districts today provide transportation for the children. If you live somewhat far from the school, and no family car is available, you depend on the school bus. Even more you depend on, and have confidence in, the—

SCHOOL BUS DRIVER

He drives his bus and picks up all . . . The boys and girls he meets . . . Along familiar country roads . . . Or on the city streets . . . He carries them to school and back . . . The whole scholastic year . . . And they get on and off without . . . The slightest doubt or fear . . . Because they know that he knows his . . . Responsibility . . . And he is careful at the wheel . . . As anyone can be . . . He loves to hear their laughter and . . . The chatter they unload . . . But first of all he tries to keep . . . His eyes upon the road . . . He is their special guardian . . . Before and after school . . . With caution and adherence to . . . Each golden traffic rule.

There are those human beings, notably women, who worry about their weight, and who will pursue almost any dietary formula to achieve or maintain a slim figure. Some do it under medical advice, to preserve their health. Others are concerned about their personal appearance. On the other side of the picture there are those who just relax and enjoy being—

FAT AND COMFORTABLE

Some people fret and worry and . . . They check their weight each day . . . While some are fat and comfortable . . . And like it just that way . . . It all depends on how they feel . . . And to a fair degree . . . It also is a question of . . . Their special vanity . . . Of course they can be sloppy fat . . . And ugly overweight . . . And wholly unconcerned about . . . The picture they create . . . But some are simply jolly round . . . And have a pleasant poise . . . And they can be quite popular . . . With all the girls and boys . . . They do not sigh about their size . . . And usually their kind . . . Is in a much more peaceful state . . . And happy frame of mind.

April 14

"He that is without sin among you—let him cast the first stone."
"Judge not, that you may not be judged." "People who live in glass
houses should not throw stones." These and other admonitions have
been handed down to us through the years, and yet we are only too
ready to condemn another. The next time you have this opportunity,
stop and think—

BEFORE YOU BLAME

to criticize . . . What other people do . . . Con-
my faults . . . And sins belong to you . . . Con-
rtues too . . . The good points they possess . . .
rs are more than theirs . . . Of equal count or
is easy to condemn . . . And now and then a
judge another person by . . . Your own peculiar
t who are you to take apart . . . And try to weigh
of other creatures like yourself . . . Who walk
. . . Be not too quick to cast a stone . . . At
to pass . . . They may return it, and your home
use of glass.

April 15

me I get blamed for things I did not do. Naturally
n I get to thinking about how much my wife does
ildren, and how much she means to us, I don't
ame. I am willing to concede she is—

MY FAULTLESS WIFE

scious of my faults . . . And how each one has
he is unaware of those . . . That could be called
eems I always get the blame . . . When anything
And it is mine to swallow if . . . We are to get
urse she never makes mistakes . . . Or wanders
Because no smallest error could . . . Be anything
but mine . . . But sometimes I incline to think . . . That maybe
she is right . . . And I have no excuse at all . . . To start a family
fight . . . She does so much to help me on . . . In life's important
game . . . Why shouldn't I accept mistakes . . . And gladly take
the blame?

nich
n the
will
-wide
agen-
coop-
ion in

which its stored than to anything on which it's poured.

Anger is an acid that can do more harm to the vessel in

—Baptist Beacon

——oOo——

got this way.

corder Sunday. Whoa! That's the way we

for one to

The WORD and WAY

OFFICIAL JOURNAL OF THE MISSOURI BAPTIST CON...

One test of true love is how you feel when you are away from your spouse. You are a traveling husband, or you are the wife who leaves town to visit relatives or friends. In that temporary separation do you experience a sense of relief and freedom, or are you sometimes—

LONELY ALONE

The more we are together, dear . . . The more my life is yours . . . The more I hold you in my arms . . . The more my love endures . . . Each moment is a memory . . . When we must be apart . . . To make more clear the image that . . . I carry in my heart . . . I am so lonely when I leave . . . So much in need of you . . . There is no happiness for me . . . In anything I do . . . Except as I am lucky in . . . The progress that I make . . . Towards joy and comfort in this life . . . For your beloved sake . . . I cherish you and love you, dear . . . I want you for my own . . . And when I have to be away . . . I am so all alone.

Prayer is our strongest fortification against sin. No one can help us as much as God Himself, with His loving grace and guidance from day to day. We ought to pray as often as possible. It need not be a lengthy prayer. Just a brief thought will do—just the simple words—

BE WITH ME, GOD

Be with me, God, in all my thoughts . . . And in the dreams I dream . . . In all the traffic of the world . . . Whatever be its scheme . . . Let not my selfishness prevail . . . In anything I do . . . Let not my soul be turned against . . . Obedience to You . . . May I be just to everyone . . . And merciful and kind . . . As every dollar that is lost . . . I hope I never find . . . I only want to serve You, God . . . In every way I can . . . And be of comfort and of help . . . To every fellow man . . . Be with me, God, and help me keep . . . The promises I make . . . Not for my earthly future but . . . For Your beloved sake.

Bosses can be mean and overbearing, and I must admit to having disliked more than one of the many for whom I worked. But also as time went by I began to realize that there were some whom I did not fully appreciate. Behind that seemingly cold frown may be—

OUR FRIEND—THE BOSS

Our friends are usually the ones . . . With whom we lunch or play . . . And seldom do we think of him . . . Who is our boss today . . . The one for whom we work, that we . . . May win our daily bread . . . And who must weigh our value and . . . Our chance to get ahead . . . We fear him and respect him, to . . . Achieve our business end . . . And almost never realize he . . . Is our devoted friend . . . And yet he has been interested . . . Right from the very start . . . And constantly he strives to keep . . . Our welfare in his heart . . . He may not always show it but . . . He knows that his success . . . Depends upon his friendship on . . . Our road to happiness.

So few crimes go unsolved that the criminal is playing a losing game, a game in which the odds are overwhelmingly against him. Then why do lawbreakers continue to operate, and why does the crime rate rise sharply now and then? It is because they cannot be convinced by words or statistics. They have to learn the hard way that there is—

NO PAY IN CRIME

In these efficient, wide-awake . . . And scientific times . . . The criminals have little chance . . . To get away with crimes . . . There are the phone and teletype . . . The radio P.D. . . . And all the experts in the field . . . Of criminology . . . The FBI, the sheriff and . . . Policeman on his beat . . . Who has been taught to use his brains . . . As well as hands and feet . . . There are so many ways in which . . . A felon can be caught . . . He ought to give the lawful life . . . A lot more sober thought . . . Our law-enforcement system is . . . So competent today . . . It should be obvious to all . . . That crime can never pay.

"All work and no play makes Jack a dull boy." It can also make him a dead boy. I once knew the head of a large firm who insisted on personally checking every business detail, although he could have delegated much of that responsibility to loyal and capable employees. He died a young man. Other persons just want to make more money faster. Greedy or overly conscientious, it is the story of—

HURRY-WORRY

A man grows old not only by . . . His years in any town . . . But equally and more because . . . His problems weigh him down . . . The older he becomes each year . . . The more he has to worry . . . The more it seems the clock of life . . . Is ticking in a hurry . . . It seems to be a race between . . . The moments that are free . . . And those that spell the letters in . . . Responsibility . . . If only he could take the time . . . To play a little longer . . . His body and his mind and heart . . . Would be a little stronger . . . But ever higher are the goals . . . That his ambition sets . . . And staying young and healthy is . . . The thing that he forgets.

However seldom I see them, I love my friends. It matters not to me whether they are rich or poor, as long as they are constant to our mutual feeling of the heart. Always and ever—

THEY ARE MY FRIENDS

My friends are all the people who . . . Remember me today . . . However long they have been gone . . . However far away . . . However recently we met . . . Upon a common street . . . Or in their palaces of gold . . . With jewels at their feet . . . It matters not how rich or poor . . . How famous or obscure . . . As long as there is friendship that . . . Is likely to endure . . . The faithful hand that reaches out . . . In loving sympathy . . . The sunny smile, the open door . . . To welcome company . . . My friends are those who send me cards . . . Or call me on the phone . . . Or in some other way make sure . . . I do not feel alone.

Spring to me is everything beautiful and wonderful that I can wish for the one I love. It is the season of hope and promise—the season of my special hope for her happiness in every loving promise that I renew. In every thought, in every dream she is—

MY SONG OF SPRING

My hopes are yours, my dreams and all . . . My every wish can bring . . . Of beauty and of happiness . . . To decorate your spring . . . The sunshine and the flowers and . . . The birds that wing the sky . . . The clean, fresh air and all the winds . . . That gently wander by . . . The smiling moon, the silver stars . . . That twinkle in the night . . . The wisdom of tomorrow in . . . A new and brighter light . . . And to my wishes, hopes and dreams . . . I add my fervent prayers . . . That God will bless you every day . . . And lighten all your cares . . . This is my song of spring for you . . . However poor my art . . . And with its humble melody . . . I offer you my heart.

The family picture is a whole album of memories. It is a record of age and size, the way we dressed, and when and where the picture was taken. Fortunate indeed are the folks who have a virtual library of family portraits. We are not so lucky, but one day—before our children were "too much" grown—we managed to get us all together, and we treasure that—

FAMILY PICTURE

We ought to have a picture made . . . Of all our family . . . To supplement our album and . . . Amuse posterity . . . But nothing is more difficult . . . In any kind of weather . . . Than trying to corral the tribe . . . And getting us together . . . The only time this special goal . . . Is one we can achieve . . . Is when our Jimmie comes ashore . . . And home on Navy leave . . . And then his sister, Kris, has friends . . . Who constantly are calling . . . And brother Don is on the field . . . With foot- or basket-balling . . . It would be wonderful to have . . . A family parade . . . If only we could get us all . . . To have our picture made.

The world is large and vast until we travel by air, and then it seems to grow smaller and smaller. But it never occurs to us how little our globe really is until we look up at the sky and compare our realm to the universe. And as we think of The Creator of all things, we begin to wonder—

HOW SMALL THE WORLD?

We meet a friend in some far place . . . Or get a sudden call . . . And then we tell each other it's . . . A small world, after all . . . Indeed the world is smaller than . . . We ever stop to think . . . Considering the universe . . . And every little link . . . Considering the sun and moon . . . That God alone designed . . . And all the stars and planets that . . . Are creatures of His mind . . . And so as we reflect upon . . . Our fame and our success . . . When we compare them with His works . . . Our height is ever less . . . The world against the universe . . . Is small as it can be . . . So think how smaller on this earth . . . Is our humanity.

A newspaper editor's job is tough but how about the problems that face the woman's editor? She must deal almost exclusively with her own sex, and you know how jealous women can be. Good reporting is not enough. On the distaff side she has to be the goddess of diplomacy. It isn't easy to be the—

WOMAN'S EDITOR

She handles all the features that . . . The women want to read . . . Advice, suggestions, helpful hints . . . And some they do not need . . . The latest styles and fashions that . . . Milady likes to wear . . . And how to brighten up her face . . . Her fingernails and hair . . . She plans the page or section to . . . Produce that dainty tone . . . And usually she also writes . . . A column of her own. . . Society and gossip notes . . . Are part of her array . . . The garden clubs, the needlecraft . . . And what to eat today . . . She has to be a journalist . . . And quite a diplomat . . . With ingenuity to please . . . The princess and the cat.

"All that glitters is not gold." This expression applies as much to people as to precious metals or stones. Some individuals are perfect diamonds, with hearts of true gold, as they live for others and are content to "get along." Others are selfish, interested only in their own gain. They are not—

GENUINE

Some people are ambitious in . . . Their own and selfish way . . . And some desire just enough . . . To live another day . . . Another day of comfort for . . . A loving family . . . With faith and hope and courage and . . . With some security . . . There is a world of difference in . . . The way they strive to live . . . The one is only out to gain . . . The other one to give . . . It is not difficult to choose . . . Between the two of them . . . And find the imitation and . . . The one who is a gem . . . There is no gorgeous jewel that . . . Will sparkle clear and bright . . . Unless it has the quality . . . To stand the strongest light.

What really inspires you to make something of your life? What is the greatest source of your ambition, your initiative, aggressiveness and perseverance? The answer is faith. Someone believes in you. And in your heart you say, "Thank you"—

AS LONG AS I KNOW

I can not get discouraged, love . . . In what I try to do . . . As long as in my heart I know . . . I may depend on you . . . As long as you have faith in me . . . And urge me ever on . . . Beyond the shadows of the night . . . To reach a brighter dawn . . . When you believe in me, there is . . . No courage that I lack . . . And in whatever task I start . . . There is no turning back . . . I cannot walk the lonely way . . . Or weep a single tear . . . I cannot entertain a doubt . . . Or have the slightest fear . . . So please believe in me, my love . . . And I shall ever be . . . Imbued with loving gratitude . . . For your good faith in me.

We all have our preference in food, especially the main dish of a dinner. Who does not enjoy a juicy steak or some tender chicken, lamb roast, or perhaps turkey with cranberry jelly? I like them all, but I have a favorite too, and mine is the—

SEAFOOD PLATE

Capon in wine is very good . . . Filet mignon is great . . . But more than beef or chicken I . . . Enjoy the seafood plate . . . The oysters fresh from Maryland . . . The lobster born in Maine . . . Those large Louisiana shrimp . . . And fish for every brain . . . The pompano from Florida . . . King salmon from the coast . . . And Colorado rainbow trout . . . Are those I like the most . . . I never was a fisherman . . . And I may never be . . . But nothing so delights me as . . . A dinner from the sea . . . And while the cow, the hen or hog . . . My appetite will sate . . . I much prefer to feast upon . . . Some kind of seafood plate.

United States citizenship is a most treasured possession, especially when conferred, instead of inherited by birth. Born in this country, you may be inclined to take your heritage for granted. But when you become an adopted child, with equal privileges, you are keenly aware of your good fortune. You thank God you are—

NO FOREIGNER

Among our loyal people who . . . Are citizens today . . . There is no single foreigner . . . Inside the U.S.A. . . . Of course there are some women and . . . Some men who used to be . . . Before they pledged allegiance to . . . Our great democracy . . . But now they are Americans . . . However old or new . . . Because they stood before our flag . . . And gave their promise true . . . No longer are they foreigners . . . Or ever out of place . . . Regardless of their background, their . . . Religion or their race . . . To them and all our native sons . . . Who form our loyal ranks . . . We give our heartfelt praise and prayers . . . And our united thanks.

If God's will were done by all humanity, there would never be such a word as "stranger" in any language. We are all creatures of God, and we were all born upon this earth for the same multiple purpose—to worship Him, to love one another, and—

TO LIVE TOGETHER

There is no stranger on the street . . . No matter where you go . . . Each individual is one . . . You do or ought to know . . . Each person is another soul . . . However old or new . . . And as a human, he or she . . . Is common unto you . . . For we are all created by . . . The same eternal God . . . And we must live our span of years . . . Together on this sod . . . Then why not walk together now . . . In heart and mind and soul . . . And strive with one another to . . . Attain the self-same goal? . . . To live in peace and happiness . . . As long as we may be . . . And by our goodness meet again . . . In God's eternity?

Yes, I love my wife and children more than anyone or anything else on earth. But I must, and I do love God even more. God gave me my family, and He allowed my own life. My family and I are united in this thought, as we tell God—

WE DO ADORE YOU

I love You, God, much more than I . . . Could ever love myself . . . And more than all the common goods . . . Upon my worldly shelf . . . I love You more than my dear wife . . . And all our children too . . . Because their happiness and mine . . . Depend, dear God, on You . . . I love You for our home and hearth . . . Each opportunity . . . And every day on earth that brings . . . A joyful memory . . . I love You not alone because . . . I need Your help each day . . . But You are God, and I belong . . . To You in every way . . . We worship and adore You, God . . . My family and I . . . And may we be Your servants true . . . Until the day we die.

It's a funny thing about life. My wife gets mad if she thinks I give too large a tip, or if I befriend someone who claims to be in need. She tells me that I am a soft touch. But no one can fall harder for a sob story than—

MY SOFTY WIFE

If I should scratch a fender or . . . A bumper on our car . . .
My wife would say, "How reckless and . . . Incompetent you are!"
. . . But when she has an accident . . . It is a different story . . .
And I must sympathize with her . . . And feel forever sorry . . .
And that is not the half of it . . . Because the other day . . . Some
lady's car rammed into ours . . . And there were bills to pay . . .
And this dear lady offered to . . . Defray our car expenses . . . As
she could well afford to do . . . In our financial census . . . But
my dear wife was filled with love . . . And deepest sympathy . . .
And so the check for our repairs . . . Was one that came from me.

May 3

The world is going to pieces. Our way of life is practically over. Nations are at war. Our economy is upside down. Children are neglected, delinquent. Government is filled with graft and corruption. We are starving. We are gradually dying. There was never anything like this (or was there?). Somehow—

LIFE GOES ON

Each generation fears the worst . . . Will happen to its kind . . .
With suffering and misery . . . Of body and of mind . . . Each
generation thinks the world . . . Is on a downward trail . . . And
there is every evidence . . . That we are bound to fail . . . And
yet the years go by and life . . . Is very much the same . . . Except the change in modern styles . . . And some established name
. . . Our habits and our problems may . . . Appear to be quite new
. . . But basically they are the ones . . . Our fathers all went
through . . . The sun comes up, the sun goes down . . . And life
is weak or strong . . . And somehow as the days go by . . . We
seem to get along.

Do you wonder sometimes what makes you feel so much in love? Do you ascribe some of the credit to the season, the flowers, or perhaps the gems in vogue? Well, don't. If everything around you seems to be more scintillating, you are only looking at a reflection of the one you love. Your beloved is the answer—

ESPECIALLY IN MAY

I love you every hour and . . . I love you every day . . . But you are something special in . . . The happy month of May . . . Perhaps it is the lilac with . . . Its fragrance in the air . . . The lily of the valley or . . . The hawthorn everywhere . . . Perhaps it is the emerald . . . That sparkles in the sun . . . To constantly remind me, dear . . . You are my only one . . . The jewels and the petals sweet . . . May play a certain part . . . And yet they do not fully tell . . . The feeling in my heart . . . Whatever flower is in bloom . . . Or gem in vogue today . . . I only know I love you so . . . Especially in May.

We usually think of the garbage can as nothing more than a lowly container for getting rid of our trash and leftovers. It is that, all right, but sometimes its contents are more than mere trash, and sometimes even a treasure may have been dumped, intentionally or not, in that—

GARBAGE CAN

How often do we think about . . . The lowly garbage can . . . The tin receptacle for trash . . . Abandoned by a man? . . . And all the stuff discarded by . . . The mistress of the house . . . Including broken glasses and . . . Another lifeless mouse? . . . It is a common catcher for . . . The things that we throw out . . . But also it may be the well . . . Of confidence or doubt . . . There may be letters slightly read . . . Or other souvenirs . . . Among the many table scraps . . . Of cereals and tears . . . There may be love and life and hope . . . Inside that garbage can . . . The tin container of the trash . . . And of the dreams of man.

Working in an office can become very monotonous, with seemingly little chance for promotion. You feel you deserve a better break. Well, don't blame your boss. He has not forgotten you. He knows that some measure of his success, however small, depends on your—

OFFICE JOB

An office job gets tiresome . . . You work from day to day . . . And nothing seems to reconcile . . . The hours with the pay . . . You have the common thought that you . . . Deserve a little more . . . Each time you end the working day . . . And close the office door . . . You may be right, you may be wrong . . . But why not trust the boss . . . To figure out the margin of . . . His profit or his loss? . . . He may be losing money while . . . Your living is at stake . . . And while he does the best for his . . . And his employee's sake . . . But either way your heart is turned . . . Remember it is true . . . That his success depends upon . . . The trust he has in you.

When the alarm clock shatters our dreams, do we ever stop to think that God has brought us safely through another night, and is giving us another day of life? We may not be rich in money, but we have our health and our loved ones, and so many little joys. We should be grateful, but perhaps—

WE DO NOT THINK

So seldom we appreciate . . . Our life from day to day . . . The health, the love, the happiness . . . The smiles along the way . . . The grace from God that lifts us up . . . And gives us strength anew . . . To carry out the promises . . . We said that we would do . . . We simply go along our way . . . And sort of trust to luck . . . And then we gripe and grumble if . . . We suddenly get stuck . . . Whatever small misfortune or . . . The softest drop of rain . . . We always seem to be prepared . . . To murmur and complain . . . Instead of being mindful of . . . The blessings we possess . . . In all the common things each day . . . That offer happiness.

Mother is a magic word. It is the symbol of love, of undying devotion, and endless, unselfish sacrifice. Once every year we pay special tribute to her who brought us into this world, and who has loved and protected us. It is Mother's Day—

HER DAY

Today belongs to Mother dear . . . It is her special day . . . We love her and we honor her . . . In our devoted way . . . We can not ever say our thanks . . . Sufficient to her name . . . But we can add our praises to . . . Her everlasting fame . . . And she deserves the very best . . . For all that she has done . . . To form the finest character . . . In daughter and in son . . . Her sacrifices never end . . . Her words are never trite . . . And we are always happy when . . . She kisses us good night . . . God bless each mother on this earth . . . Wherever she may be . . . And keep her in His loving care . . . For all eternity.

God is so good to me. He showers me with His blessings from day to day. He teaches me to walk in His way. He lifts me when I fall. He is patient when I fail Him, ever ready to take me in His arms again. What can I do in return? Dear God, I want so much—

TO PAY YOU BACK

What have I done for You, my God . . . For all the ways You bless? . . . What have I given in return . . . For health and happiness? . . . You gave my very life to me . . . My mind and every breath . . . And all the wonders of the earth . . . From infancy to death . . . You showed me how I ought to walk . . . Among my fellow men . . . And when I faltered and I failed . . . You helped me rise again . . . How can I thank You half enough . . . Or make it up to You? . . . What sacrifice is there, my God . . . That You would have me do? . . . There are so many principles . . . And virtues that I lack . . . But in my humble, tearful way . . . I hope to pay You back.

When you are deeply in love, it matters not who proposes. Once the words are spoken, your two worlds become as one, and your smiles and tears are blended together like the colors of the rainbow, as your lips declare—

I WANT YOU TOO

You took me in your arms tonight . . . You promised to be true . . . And you implored my heart to be . . . Forever close to you . . . You said you wanted me, my dear . . . The moment that we met . . . And if you lived a hundred years . . . You never could forget . . . Well, that is how I want you, dear . . . Forever and a day . . . With all the hopes and promises . . . That I can ever say . . . And so I offer you my heart . . . And all that I can give . . . And I will live my life for you . . . Each moment that I live . . . To bring you every happiness . . . And keep away your tears . . . And walk the path of love with you . . . Through all the golden years.

Every good mother worries over the welfare and safety of her son, beginning with his earliest day in the cradle. She will face any danger to protect him, and yet—quite naturally—she does not want him to engage in anything hazardous, such as being a—

JET PILOT

His mother used to warn him not . . . To roller skate too fast . . . And when he pumped his bicycle . . . She really was aghast . . . And now he wears a uniform . . . And now he flies a jet . . . Where speed is simply something of . . . A record to be set . . . He zooms his plane across the sky . . . Above the fading ground . . . To challenge lightning flashes and . . . The swiftness that is sound . . . What happened to the roller skates? . . . And what about the bike? . . . And every other swiftness that . . . His mother did not like? . . . Let us remember there is God . . . Who knows our every need . . . Who always watches over us . . . And regulates our speed.

*Do you ever have to pack your bags in a hurry? You are going on
a business or emergency trip, and you want to have all those essential
items, but somehow something is always left out. It happens even
when you start your vacation and you have plenty of time for—*

PACKING YOUR BAGS

The stuff you need to travel with . . . Is quite a heavy haul . . .
And always you are wondering . . . If you have packed it all . . .
The suit and socks, or dress and hose . . . The toothpaste and the
brush . . . The necktie, powder or the gloves . . . When you are
in a rush . . . And then you reach the station and . . . You get
aboard the train . . . And after while you realize that . . . Your
efforts were in vain . . . You left behind your wallet, your . . .
Address book, watch or ring . . . Somehow it never seems to be . . .
Some unimportant thing . . . And if you took two dozen days . . .
To pack before you traveled . . . You still would miss some item
when . . . Your luggage you unraveled.

*A friendship, to be really worth while, must be something more
than a mere smile and handshake, or the willingness to do a favor.
It must have that spiritual aspect of moral uplift and mutual encouragement that makes it a—*

FRIENDSHIP IN GOD

There is no friendship worth our while . . . Unless we strive to
give . . . Some help to other humans in . . . The way they ought
to live . . . We must be conscious of their souls . . . As surely as
their hearts . . . And keep in mind the welfare true . . . Of all
their moral parts . . . There is no friendship on the path . . .
Where sin and Satan meet . . . As we connive for someone else
. . . To lie or steal or cheat . . . A friendship has no meaning if
. . . The end in sight is crime . . . Because its very purpose will
. . . Defeat itself in time . . . The only friendship worth our
while . . . Is helping one another . . . To keep The Lord's Commandments as . . . A sister or a brother.

No field of endeavor in this life is so crowded as to warrant our being discouraged from entering it and trying to get to the top. Competition may be strong, and the odds may seem overwhelmingly against us, but if we have the ability and the courage, there is always—

ROOM FOR ONE MORE

However crowded is the field . . . Where you would make your score . . . If you possess the talent, there . . . Is room for still one more . . . Indeed the crowd is not composed . . . Of those who reach the top . . . The crowd is at the bottom where . . . So many fail or stop . . . Who try to make a living and . . . Who earn a meager crust . . . Or those so disappointed that . . . They give up in disgust . . . In business or profession or . . . A common labor crew . . . The honored goal for which you hope . . . Is strictly up to you . . . It is not likely you will be . . . Forgotten in the crowd . . . Because your true ability . . . Will echo strong and loud.

Have you ever realized the seriousness of taking an oath? Do you know its meaning? When you raise your hand on the witness stand, or you sign an affidavit, you are calling upon God to witness the truth of your statement. You may fool your fellow man, but you cannot deceive your Creator. Therefore—

LIE NOT TO GOD

What is the meaning of an oath . . . That you decide to take . . . In your behalf or, now and then . . . For someone else's sake? . . . You sign an affidavit or . . . You take the witness stand . . . And swear that you are truthful as . . . You elevate your hand . . . It means that you are asking God . . . To witness then and there . . . That what you say or what you sign . . . Is honest, true and square . . . And if you do not tell the truth . . . Your deed is perjury . . . And as a sin against your God . . . It is a tragedy . . . Because to God your oath becomes . . . A binding obligation . . . In which there cannot be the least . . . Of mental reservation.

Sometimes I let my duties pile up from one day to another. Eventually I get them all done, but I am not happy in that process. The more I neglect my work, the more my conscience bothers me. My only true peace and satisfaction are derived from doing each thing when it should be done. I like—

TO DO MY PART

Tomorrow will be happier . . . By what I do today . . . If I accomplish something else . . . Besides a bit of play . . . If I pursue my daily task . . . And carry out my chore . . . And then on top of my routine . . . Perhaps a little more . . . The joy of recreation good . . . Is not in fun itself . . . But also in the work that I . . . Have cleared from every shelf . . . There is an inspiration true . . . In every little spark . . . And every bullet that is aimed . . . May hit a better mark . . . Tomorrow will be happier . . . And brighter than today . . . If I am conscientious as . . . I go along my way.

Many years ago this day Norway gained her independence, and ever since she has defended it courageously against all odds. Whenever war threatens the peace and security of the world—the democratic way of life—our great and freedom-loving nation may be sure to find—

NORWAY WITH US

Today is Norway's holiday . . . The time of celebration . . . When it became a country free . . . An independent nation . . . Throughout the years it has not failed . . . To keep that torch aflame . . . And no invader ever has . . . Destroyed or changed its name . . . It is the land of vikings strong . . . Where courage is the measure . . . Of human rights and all the things . . . That common people treasure . . . The flag of Norway flies today . . . Beside our banner bright . . . And always with our Stars and Stripes . . . It is prepared to fight . . . Regardless of the odds there are . . . By armament or weather . . . The sons of Norway and our sons . . . Will always be together.

Those announcements on the bulletin board and those memos passed around the office or plant are all right at times (especially if they convey good news). But constant reminders can become monotonous and time-consuming, and sometimes employees would be better off without those—

NOTES FROM THE BOSS

Our boss is one who falls in love . . . With certain things he reads . . . And feels that they are just the thoughts . . . To fill our mental needs . . . An essay or an article . . . A poem or a quip . . . Or that embarrassment that comes . . . Between the cup and lip . . . And so he has some copies made . . . And they are passed around . . . Or else as tacked-up bulletins . . . These messages abound . . . Well, some of them are interesting . . . And some are rather quaint . . . A few of them are clever and . . . A lot of others ain't . . . But now and then we tell ourselves . . . Production could be speeding . . . If we could just reduce the time . . . Devoted to our reading.

Some husbands tire of the routine of going to work every day and coming home every night. They do not realize their good fortune. Other husbands have to travel, seldom see their wives and children. Lucky indeed is the—

HUSBAND AT HOME

How many husbands ever know . . . How fortunate they are . . . That they are not required now . . . To travel very far? . . . That they just go downtown each day . . . And come home every night . . . To join the loving family . . . And know that all is right? . . . They surely should appreciate . . . The hours that are theirs . . . To be with those who mean so much . . . And tend to all their cares . . . Instead of being lonely in . . . A city far away . . . And wondering and worrying . . . And writing every day . . . There may be riches on the road . . . Wherever husbands roam . . . But nothing like the wealth of love . . . When they may be at home.

You are "going steady" with someone and because of circumstances you have to meet at a certain, special place every night—a bench in the park or a street corner. And then one night that someone isn't there. What happened? Probably nothing serious, but in your heart and in your stomach you have a feeling to match that—

EMPTY CORNER

The rain is on my windowpane . . . The sidewalk and the street
. . . I see it on the corner too . . . Where every night we meet
. . . I see it by the lamplight and . . . The headlights on the cars
. . . But you have disappeared tonight . . . As much as all the
stars . . . The rain is realistic and . . . The corner, dear, is too . . .
But all the rest is just a mist . . . A memory of you . . . I do not
mind the kind of sky . . . The cloudy or the fair . . . But what
about that corner, love . . . And why are you not there? . . . Per-
haps you could not help it and . . . There is no cause for fright
. . . And yet I wonder if you will . . . Be there tomorrow night.

*When we turn our thoughts to God and ask Him to bless some-
one, let us think especially of our spouse—the one we love, the one
who has been so good to us. Let us acknowledge our faults and failures, and our sweetheart's forbearance, as we say—*

BLESS YOU, MY LOVE

God bless you for the love and joy . . . That you have given me
. . . And bless your understanding heart . . . With all its sympathy . . . God bless you for your patience and . . . Your soft and
kindly mood . . . Your gentleness and sweetness and . . . Forgiv-
ing attitude . . . I know that I have made mistakes . . . So many
more than you . . . That all the blame is mine because . . . Our
dreams have not come true . . . And yet you keep on going, dear
. . . And never criticize . . . But hold me up to public view . . .
As something of a prize . . . God bless your every sacrifice . . .
And give me strength to be . . . A little equal to the goal . . .
Where you would honor me.

Although I have no desire to be a memory expert, I find myself annoyed at times when I meet someone whose face is so familiar that the name should come to me at once, and it doesn't. Invariably the reason is that the individual is "out of his corral." I am used to associating—

FACES AND PLACES

I meet a lot of people and . . . It is no easy thing . . . To catalog their faces and . . . To keep remembering . . . And it is even harder to . . . Recall a person's name . . . And when we meet there is no time . . . To play a guessing game . . . But what annoys me most of all . . . Is some familiar face . . . With all those friendly features that . . . I somehow cannot place . . . And later, when it comes to me . . . I know why I forgot . . . It was because I met him where . . . He usually is not . . . I think I would remember each . . . Familiar smile and face . . . If only everyone remained . . . In his accustomed place.

The hanger is probably the most useful nuisance ever created. It certainly is useful for hanging up suits and dresses, and preserving their presses, but when you reach for one and try to yank it out of the closet, you have a battle on your hands. You are up against the—

HANGER

The hangers in my closet are . . . Convenient as can be . . . But sometimes they are only there . . . To test my sanity . . . I struggle for a hanger as . . . I reach inside the door . . . And soon they are a tangled bunch . . . That rests upon the floor . . . I reach for one that I believe . . . Will have the problem solved . . . But when I try to yank it out . . . I find myself involved . . . It snags into another and . . . It simply won't let go . . . And when it does, it catapults . . . And gives me quite a blow . . . The hanger has its purpose but . . . It sure is hard to choose . . . And when I try to pick one out . . . It is the war I lose.

Life is filled with memories, and so is mine. I can recall my early childhood, and thousands of scenes and thoughts and words since then. But the really important memories are those I share with the one I love—those that belong to us alone and together. In that sense they are—

MY ONLY MEMORIES

I have no memories beyond . . . The hours spent with you . . . The day we met, the night we kissed . . . And promised to be true . . . The weeks, the months, the seasons and . . . The years we lived together . . . Whatever disappointments and . . . However bad the weather . . . I have no memories beyond . . . The moments that we shared . . . With smiling eyes and whispered words . . . To tell how much we cared . . . No other memories could meet . . . Their full and perfect measure . . . And they will always be my own . . . To dream about and treasure . . . And I will always be your own . . . As much as you were mine . . . In every song, in every prayer . . . And every grateful line.

As you grew in childhood, you were allowed gradually to stay up later and later at night. And there was that first New Year's Eve when you heard the clock strike midnight. You thought it was fun. Today the bewitching hour may mean nothing to you, but any doctor will tell you to be in bed before midnight if you want to get—

A GOOD NIGHT'S SLEEP

The hours after midnight may . . . Be memories to keep . . . But there is nothing better than . . . To get a good night's sleep . . . There is a feeling of romance . . . When stars are wide awake . . . And lips may come together or . . . A lonely heart may break . . . And there may be a business deal . . . To worry and upset . . . The proud, ambitious mind of man . . . In what it wants to get . . . But sleep is more important to . . . The welfare of the day . . . And to the health and strength of all . . . Our labor and our play . . . And as there is a time to sow . . . And then a time to reap . . . So let us put away the day . . . And get a good night's sleep.

Most people are content to do their daily jobs in the usual, satis-
factory way. Others go beyond the call of duty. They give that some-
thing extra—that part of themselves—to serve their community. They
go out of their way to be kind and helpful, like the

COUNTRY POSTMASTER

The ones who supervise the mail . . . In any little town . . .
Deserve their recognition and . . . Perhaps a special crown . . .
The postmaster and mistress who . . . Are always right on hand
. . . To answer every question and . . . To meet the least demand
. . . They read to folks and help them write . . . The words they
want to say . . . And sometimes wrap the packages . . . That peo-
ple send away . . . They even lend the pennies for . . . The
stamps that some can't buy . . . And gladly fill the fountain pens
. . . That suddenly run dry . . . They are as friendly and as kind
. . . As anyone can be . . . These women and these men who
serve . . . Their small community.

Time seems to be so important in our way of life. We rise by the
alarm clock. We follow the hands of our watch as we rush to school
or work, or to keep special appointments. But who cares when the
night is young, with moon and stars above, and love surrounds our
hearts? How can there be any—

MATTER OF TIME

The clock is quite an instrument . . . It tells the time of day . . .
And whether we should be at work . . . Or have a chance to play
. . . It regulates the schoolroom and . . . The home and factory
. . . And everywhere by day or night . . . Where everyone should
be . . . It checks the train, the bus and plane . . . The trolley on
the street . . . And every transportation with . . . A schedule it
must meet . . . The clock is like a guardian . . . That tells us
what to do . . . The time we should begin a task . . . And when
we should get through . . . Except when love has wound the clock
. . . With rhythm and with rhyme . . . Then nothing on this
earth can be . . . As meaningless as time.

What is a prayer? It is a conversation with God. We thank Him for His blessings, we tell Him our troubles, and we ask His grace and guidance. It is just like talking to any friend, except that our words are being addressed to our dearest Friend, and He will never fail us. His help is our answer—

SO LET US PRAY

Why should it be so difficult . . . To turn to God and pray? . . . Why should we stammer in our hearts . . . Or grope for words to say? . . . We talk to relatives and friends . . . At home or on the street . . . And many are the strangers whom . . . We courteously greet . . . But here is God, our closest Friend . . . Who helps us so much more . . . Than all the other visitors . . . Who knock upon our door . . . And He is not particular . . . About the way we speak . . . Though always ready to fulfill . . . The favor that we seek . . . So let us pray as we would talk . . . To any faithful friend . . . And leave our troubles in His hands . . . To bring them to their end.

Has it happened to you? One day, without warning, your loved one seems different, apart from you. You wonder if you are to blame, if you have done something wrong. The air is silent. Your heart is disturbed. Your mind is puzzled, as you tell your sweetheart—

I CRIED TONIGHT

I cried tonight, with all the tears . . . That I could offer you . . . And in my silent loneliness . . . I wish you really knew . . . I cried because there may have been . . . Some way I made you sad . . . Or something I neglected, dear . . . That might have made you glad . . . My tears were not the nervous ones . . . Of sorrow or distress . . . But just my innermost concern . . . About your happiness . . . I cried because I met you and . . . I called your loving name . . . And somehow in the starlight, dear . . . You did not look the same . . . I hope that I was wrong, dear one . . . As much as I could be . . . And I am still your own, and you . . . Are still in love with me.

We call it Memorial Day because we commemorate our soldier dead. We call it Decoration Day because we decorate their graves with flags and flowers, and because our brave departed deserve more than all the decorations we could give. Although a holiday, it is no time for celebration. It is the occasion to bow our heads and pray for—

OUR SOLDIER DEAD

God rest the dead, our soldier dead . . . Who died for you and me . . . And bless them for their faith and love . . . And for their bravery . . . The ones who gave their all for us . . . Upon the battlefield . . . Because they had convictions and . . . Because they would not yield . . . They were the wall of our defense . . . They held the crucial front . . . Whatever battle they were in . . . They always bore the brunt . . . They are the heroes in the hall . . . Of everlasting fame . . . Where no one in the realm of God . . . Has any greater claim . . . For they laid down their lives for us . . . And who can offer more . . . To serve his God and fellow man . . . On any sea or shore?

The school bell rings louder than ever before. Childish shouts and laughter fill the air, as little legs dash through the door to freedom. Classes are over—summer vacation is here! It's wonderful, but also it is the time when parents become more anxious, and when they pray—

GOD KEEP THEM SAFE

It is that time of year and life . . . The very last of May . . . When schools are just about to close . . . And youngsters turn to play . . . Perhaps another week or two . . . Or maybe even three . . . Depending on the climate and . . . The school board policy . . . But when the classrooms vanish and . . . The children swim and fish . . . May all their days be happy and . . . Their parents get their wish . . . That God will keep them safe from harm . . . Wherever they may be . . . To let them go on living and . . . Preserve the family . . . And bring them back to school again . . . Refreshed and gay and well . . . To keep their noses in their books . . . And answer every bell.

Wonderful June! The open door to summer, with sunshine flowers, it is the month of happiness, laughter and love. Wedding bells are ringing, brides are blushing, and everything of life is beautiful. What is more wonderful than—

WONDERFUL JUNE

I love each day of every week . . . Along the month of June . . . The clear blue sky, the sun on high . . . And every golden moon . . . I love the honeysuckle and . . . The rose so sweet and fair . . . The sailboats on the water and . . . The romance in the air . . . The wanderlust that beckons me . . . To highway, dale and wood . . . The laughter of the children in . . . Their happy neighborhood . . . It is the time for wedding bells . . . And loving hearts that blend . . . With hopes and dreams of home and hearth . . . In vows that never end . . . The month of June is wonderful . . . I wish that it would last . . . As long as all the months of June . . . Together in the past.

June 2

Letters of love are part of every romance. We keep them, we treasure them, and we read them over and over. Messages of love, on cards or stationery, are the thoughts of our hearts that so often we write when we have not the voice to express them face to face. I save each note. I hoard each word in—

MY SPECIAL BOX

I keep your loving letters in . . . A special box of mine . . . With all your pretty greeting cards . . . And every valentine . . . Each message you have sent me, dear . . . Has been a flower fair . . . To brighten all my hours and . . . To tell me that you care . . . Especially when skies are sad . . . And I am feeling blue . . . And in my lonely heart I wish . . . That I could be with you . . . I read your letters over and . . . I kiss each card you sent . . . Because I know that every word . . . Is one you really meant . . . And every time I touch my box . . . I pray the time will be . . . When I can listen to your lips . . . And hold you close to me.

Water is good for you. You should drink plenty of it every day. But watch your drinking habits if you work in an office or plant. The boss may get the wrong impression if he sees you lingering at that—

WATER COOLER

The water cooler is the place . . . Where office people gather . . . To say the things their boss might hear . . . But wish he would not, rather . . . Where gossip bubbles, dates are made . . . And funny stories told . . . The bets on boxing bouts are laid . . . And party plans unfold . . . It is the common meeting ground . . . For soft and furtive chatter . . . About the daily happenings . . . That do not really matter . . . Where time and cups are wasted in . . . The basket just below . . . And few are truly thirsty when . . . They make the water flow . . . But many are the bosses who . . . Are constantly surmising . . . That those who hang around the trough . . . Are not so enterprising.

It's wonderful to call on friends, lose ourselves in conversation with them, and thrive on their hospitality. Those are moments that are never to be forgotten. But somehow I enjoy their company even more when they are my guests. I feel happier when I can entertain them when I go—

TO VISIT FRIENDS

I always like to visit friends . . . Wherever they may be . . . To step into their homes and share . . . Their hospitality . . . Around the closest corner or . . . A thousand miles away . . . With wonderful companionship . . . To pass the time of day . . . Perhaps to stay for dinner or . . . A glass of tea with ice . . . But mostly conversation that . . . Is neighborly and nice . . . I long to learn their problems in . . . The manner that they live . . . And try to share my life with them . . . As much as I can give . . . I like to visit all my friends . . . Wherever they may be . . . But even more I do implore . . . To have them visit me.

How much are you in love with your spouse and children? Do you sacrifice your comfort and convenience for them? Is there nothing that you would not do for them? Then, surely, you also overlook their faults and shortcomings, and you ask God—

GIVE ME THE BLAME

If there must be a shadow, God . . . Let it envelop me . . . And never touch the members of . . . My loving family . . . If any sort of sacrifice . . . Or punishment is due . . . Please call on me and no one else . . . To make it up to You . . . I pray that they will never weep . . . Or know the smallest strife . . . And for their earthly happiness . . . I offer You my life . . . I offer You the heart and soul . . . That You have given me . . . And every penance I can do . . . Throughout eternity . . . Protect them, God, and guide them to . . . That everlasting goal . . . And if they make an error, let . . . The sin be on my soul.

There are two kinds of warmth, the outer and the inner. The body may be warmed by the sun, a blanket, a tepid bath or other means. That is outer warmth. It comforts the physical being but not the spiritual. Only love can bring joy and peace to the soul, whether it comes from God or the earthly object of your affection. So, tell that someone: Thank you, my love, for—

THE WARMTH OF YOU

The air is warm today, my love . . . Not by the summer sun . . . But just because I know you are . . . My one and only one . . . And that is why my heart is warm . . . And cozy as can be . . . Because in all the world you are . . . The dearest one to me . . . And if it were in wintertime . . . With ice and sleet and snow . . . There still would be the comfort of . . . That warm, familiar glow . . . I find no temperature too hot . . . No temperature too cold . . . The air is always soothing when . . . You are my own to hold . . . It is the feeling of your arms . . . The sweetness of your lips . . . And all the warmth that tingles to . . . My very fingertips.

*We may use it dozens of times a day, yet seldom appreciate its use-
fulness. Although specially processed, and capable of performing
many services, it is usually relegated to the job of soaking up wet ink.
It is that ordinary—*

BLOTTER

A blotter is an instrument . . . That serves to soak up ink . . .
And that may smear but cannot change . . . The written words you
think . . . It dries the fluid from your pen . . . To leave your letter
neat . . . Or make it slightly easier . . . To change or to delete
. . . But also it can well record . . . Your writing in reverse . . .
And with a common mirror it . . . Can make your troubles worse
. . . A blotter also helps to lift . . . The stains from rug and floor
. . . And as for household uses, it . . . Has many, many more . . .
But while it is a helping hand . . . And gives you many breaks . . .
Remember that no blotter now . . . Can blot out your mistakes.

*Some people are constantly complaining about their surroundings
—the city, community, or part of the country in which they are making their home. They don't like the climate. They think their neighbors are stupid. They are always comparing notes with the "better"
places where they have resided. But living—living with others—really
matters—*

NOT WHERE—BUT HOW

It does not matter where you live . . . But how you spend your
day . . . That really brings you happiness . . . In all your work
and play . . . The weather may be terrible . . . The sun may
never rise . . . And rain and wind or snow and sleet . . . May
sweep down from the skies . . . The day may be the hottest or . . .
The coldest of the year . . . But it can be a perfect one . . . Depending on your cheer . . . Depending on your friendly smile . . .
To neighbors here and there . . . And your most willing helpfulness . . . To people everywhere . . . And as you try to live for
them . . . So they will live for you . . . And you will find your joy
in all . . . The kindly things you do.

If a poll were taken, it is not unlikely that the most popular room in any house would turn up to be the kitchen. Even a baby knows that. He knows where his food is prepared, and when he acquires the use of his limbs, he toddles out there and reaches up for jam and cookies. The older he gets, the more he likes the—

KITCHEN

The kitchen is the place to cook . . . And wash the dirty dishes . . . And keep the food that satisfies . . . The husband's hungry wishes . . . The room that has the sweetest smell . . . By any day or night . . . According to capacity . . . And special appetite . . . Where Junior gets his breakfast and . . . His mom prepares the dinner . . . And every cake and every pie . . . Becomes another winner . . . The kitchen is the special spot . . . To get that midnight snack . . . In every palace beautiful . . . And every humble shack . . . It is that most inviting place . . . Where people get together . . . When they are not too much concerned . . . About their waistline measure.

Have you ever listened to the wind? Does it seem to whisper to you? Sometimes it has a haunting sound, like a voice out of the past. You think you hear someone speaking. It sounds familiar, yet strange, and you wonder if it is a message—

OR JUST THE WIND?

Is that your whisper in the wind . . . That shakes my contemplation? . . . Or is it just another sound . . . In my imagination? . . . I thought I heard your loving voice . . . And that you said to me . . . I am the only one on earth . . . In all your memory . . . Is it a little possible . . . That in my lonely hour . . . Such fragrance would imbue again . . . This pressed and faded flower? . . . But, no, the night is dark and cold . . . And there is only space . . . I cannot touch your hand or see . . . The outline of your face . . . It must be just my weary mind . . . Or something in the weather . . . And yet the wind keeps whispering . . . As though we were together.

Our best prayer to God is our silent prayer. It is the prayer that comes sincerely from the heart. It need not be composed of words. In truth, our deeds can speak more eloquently our love for Him and our desire to do His will. The important thing is the humble sincerity of all—

WHO PRAY TO GOD

God's humble people are the ones . . . Who take the time to pray . . . Whose words to Him are silent ones . . . That they sincerely say . . . Who make no spectacle in church . . . For everyone to see . . . How saintly and devotional . . . Their actions seem to be . . . Whose prayers are not just Sunday prayers . . . That everyone can hear . . . As voices echo through the church . . . And tones are loud and clear . . . But who remember God at home . . . In town and everywhere . . . With never any audience . . . To hear their fervent prayer . . . And every morning, noon and night . . . They surely are sincere . . . Because their thoughts and prayers are those . . . That only God can hear.

There are some tests you can pass in a matter of minutes—in school or business—and the passing mark becomes a permanent credit. But there is one test that goes on day after day, and your passing grade can come only a day at a time. It is the—

FRIENDSHIP TEST

A friend may last forever or . . . For just a little while . . . According to the measure and . . . The warmness of his smile . . . According to his faith and trust . . . His heartfelt sympathy . . . And all the noble virtues that . . . Comprise integrity . . . Or by his sudden weakness in . . . The hour of your strife . . . And his affection for his own . . . Convenience in this life . . . It all depends on whether he . . . Can pass the friendship test . . . With readiness and willingness . . . To give his very best . . . And if he ever fails you once . . . You may be certain then . . . He will not change his character . . . Or be your friend again.

As much as death and taxes are certain, so the survey is uncertain. It is based on a sample—but what of the sample? It may be right or wrong. What kind of sample was taken? How was it taken? Was there a motive? It can be a guide, but there never is certainty in the—

SURVEY

The survey is a way in which . . . To take the pulse of life . . . And study its reaction to . . . Our struggle and our strife . . . It is a poll of public thought . . . In some selected field . . . To see what answers and ideas . . . The inquiry may yield . . . It may be fairly accurate . . . Or it may miss the boat . . . According to the way in which . . . We gather in the vote . . . It must be taken carefully . . . And in the final grade . . . There ought to be some margin for . . . Mistakes that may be made . . . The survey may report in fact . . . The views we all express . . . Or it may be the wasteful work . . . Of just another guess.

Today is Flag Day. It is the day set aside to honor our flag—the American Flag, Old Glory, the Stars and Stripes. As we look upon this symbol of our heritage and of "the Republic for which it stands, one nation under God, indivisible, with liberty and justice for all," let us—

SALUTE AND PRAY

Let everyone salute our flag . . . And say a prayer today . . . That God will always help us keep . . . Our democratic way . . . Let us give gratitude to Him . . . For our United States . . . With justice and equality . . . And freedom from all hates . . . With liberty to live our lives . . . In peace and unity . . . And to protect our human rights . . . And worldly property . . . Let us salute the Stars and Stripes . . . Our great red, white and blue . . . And give again our solemn pledge . . . To be forever true . . . And let us pray to God today . . . That we shall never lag . . . In cherishing and fighting for . . . Our own, beloved flag.

June is the month of love. It is the traditional month for brides. But June has ears for more than wedding bells. There are the chimes of new engagements, and there is always the hopeful melody of—

OUR HEARTS IN JUNE

In June I love the whole wide world . . . And all the flowers too . . . But when it comes to human love . . . My heart belongs to you . . . In every ray of sunshine and . . . In every petal bright . . . I whisper my good morning and . . . I say a sweet good night . . . My lips are yours, and your soft eyes . . . Are all I want to see . . . And in your loving arms I hold . . . My every memory . . . What is the answer in your heart . . . Beneath the sun and moon? . . . Will you be mine forever, dear . . . This happy day in June? . . . Tell me the truth, whatever else . . . I may have heard or seen . . . Give me your heart and whisper now . . . The words you really mean.

It is a common trait to think that we are worth more than we are being paid. Maybe we are, maybe not. But is it not better to be worth more than we get, than to get more than we are worth? Of course, there can be the happy medium for which we all hope, and that is what the average boss is always striving for. He wants to balance the—

PAYROLL

The payroll is a list of names . . . Of persons who get paid . . . According to mentality . . . Ability and grade . . . According to the work they do . . . Or what they seem to know . . . Production that is over par . . . Precisely, or below . . . Of course some may be worth above . . . The envelope they clutch . . . While others on the payroll may . . . Be getting much too much . . . But he who strives to figure what . . . The payroll ought to be . . . Is usually a human judge . . . With good economy . . . He gives the most he can to those . . . Employees who excel . . . And tries to give a break to those . . . Who do not do so well.

You cannot see God but your heart can commune with Him. You can tell Him your troubles and your hopes and dreams. And if you listen closely, you can hear Him speaking to you. You can hear His voice in the consoling reaction of your prayers, in the knowledge that He is always at your side. Yes—

GOD SPEAKS TO YOU

God speaks to you in His own way . . . Or have you never heard . . . His kind, consoling message and . . . The wisdom of His word? . . . He speaks of love and brotherhood . . . And courage in your strife . . . Of faith and deep humility . . . And virtue in this life . . . His voice is not the common kind . . . The sound from lips that part . . . It is a sweet and gentle tongue . . . That whispers to your heart . . . It does not scold or criticize . . . Or make the least demand . . . It only wants to let you know . . . That God will understand . . . God speaks to you each day and night . . . His voice is soft but clear . . . And you will hear His word unless . . . You do not want to hear.

Some people may decry the commercial aspects of Mother's Day and Father's Day, the promotion to stimulate sales in various stores. But if these observances do nothing else, they more than justify themselves by serving to remind us of God's Fourth Commandment. Indeed every day should be her and—

HIS DAY

We set this day aside to give . . . Our gratitude and praise . . . To one who is so generous . . . Yet silent in his ways . . . The father of the family . . . The master of the house . . . Whose voice may be atomic but . . . Is heard just like a mouse . . . Who likes to think he is the boss . . . But always is on hand . . . To do the greatest favor or . . . To meet the least demand . . . He has to match his monthly pay . . . With all the bills there are . . . Including life insurance and . . . The upkeep of a car . . . And as he tries to do his best . . . According to his way . . . May God be extra good to him . . . On this his Father's Day.

Marriage binds two hearts together but it is not the official stamp of true love. It is merely a ceremony, albeit a sacred one. True love is in the heart and soul. It exists before and during the marriage, and it continues to exist, even though the marriage may die. It is that something within me when I say—

SO MUCH MY LOVE

Our marriage is a contract and . . . As legal as can be . . . I am your own forever, dear . . . And you belong to me . . . You have your every right to me . . . As much as you are mine . . . And we belong together by . . . Each promise and each sign . . . But if there were no contract and . . . There were no marriage true . . . I still would love your heart and have . . . The same respect for you . . . I merely want to tell you, love . . . You mean so much to me . . . That I belong to you and God . . . For all eternity . . . And even if you changed your mind . . . About the way you care . . . You would remain forever in . . . My every thought and prayer.

Most of us have so many friends that we could not possibly contact all of them every day. The knowledge that we have them, and that usually we can reach them at any time is comforting, but we should not let too many weeks or months slip by. Now and then we ought—

TO KEEP IN TOUCH

My friends are scattered here and there . . . It does not really matter . . . While we can keep in touch by mail . . . Or other means to chatter . . . As long as I have filed away . . . Each name and each address . . . Or where to call by telephone . . . And wish them happiness . . . Of course I wish that every day . . . No matter what the weather . . . My friends could say hello to me . . . And we could be together . . . But just a little greeting card . . . Will turn that happy trick . . . It need not be a telegram . . . Or any message quick . . . Whatever and however is . . . The message I may send them . . . It matters only as I try . . . To cheer and to befriend them.

Summer is here. This is the season of warmth and fun, the
of year when most families go on vacation. It is another po
the calendar that God created for the variation of human int
nature. Let us enjoy it, and—

THANK GOD FOR SUMMER

Thank God for summer every year . . . With warmth and sunshine bright . . . A golden moon and silver stars . . . To light the
way at night . . . The joyful season when the earth . . . Is in its
fullest bloom . . . With happy hours by the clock . . . But never
time for gloom . . . The flowers in the city park . . . The sailboats
on the sea . . . The clover in the meadow and . . . Each youthful
reverie . . . The county fair, the picnic and . . . The hammock
on the lawn . . . The swimming and the fishing and . . . The
many goings-on . . . Thank God we have the summertime . . . To
rest and to relax . . . And drift in dreams to fairyland . . . Away
from worldly facts.

June 22

Whenever you think you are Mr. Big, just take a look in the mir-
ror. Does it reflect a greatness that comes from you or from another
source—perhaps from God? Look in the mirror, not the one in your
bathroom or on the wall of some resplendent building, but the—

MIRROR OF YOUR HEART

How much are you a genius true? . . . How brilliant is your star?
. . . Look in the mirror and behold . . . How wonderful you are
. . . Consider not your wide acclaim . . . According to your art
. . . But search for that reflection in . . . The mirror of your heart
. . . How do you feel about yourself . . . And what they say you
do? . . . Are you deserving of the praise . . . Your public gives to
you? . . . Or could it be that someone else . . . Should have that
honored role? . . . Perhaps The One Who gave you life . . . And
helped you gain your goal? . . . Look in the mirror of your heart
. . . Where truth can never hide . . . And you will find reflected
there . . . Your humbleness or pride.

[95]

How much and how long are we in love? It all depends. Love may be for now or forever. We may have an "understanding," or we may be engaged. Either may be dissolved without serious consequence to the soul. But when the sacred vows of matrimony are exchanged, love is for life—

WITH YOU FOREVER

I dream of you, I cherish you . . . Each second of each hour . . . To me you are the petals and . . . The fragrance of each flower . . . You are the silver stars that are . . . The sentinels of night . . . You are the dawn when fear is gone . . . You are my sunshine bright . . . You are the hopes that fill my heart . . . In all their fullest measure . . . You are the one and only one . . . I ever want to treasure . . . To you I give my loving heart . . . My life for evermore . . . With all the joys I own today . . . And all that are in store . . . I only want your happiness . . . Forever and forever . . . I only want to be with you . . . And never leave you—never.

Is God in your heart? Is He with you every moment of every day and night? Do you remember Him and thank Him when life is happy and carefree? Do you turn to Him in time of trouble and need? He is always there to comfort you. He loves to hear you say—

BE IN MY HEART

Dear God, be in my heart today . . . And fill my every need . . . Inspire me to honor You . . . In thought and word and deed . . . Let not my mind be weakened now . . . By selfishness or wrath . . . Let not my tongue be idle or . . . My footsteps lose the path . . . But help me to remember all . . . The graces You bestow . . . My health, my home, my comfort and . . . My friend who says hello . . . The wind and rain, the sunshine and . . . The stars and flowers bright . . . And every opportunity . . . To stand for what is right . . . Dear God, be in my heart today . . . With strength and will to live . . . With faith and hope eternal and . . . The charity to give.

*A family, by the commonest definition, is a husband and wife,
and a child or children. But the word "family," in the eyes of God,
has a much more important meaning. It is the way they live together,
love one another, and strive for their welfare and the welfare of their
neighbors. That is the test of the—*

TRUE FAMILY

What really makes a family . . . And keeps it all together? . . .
It is not just the home and hearth . . . And surely not the weather
. . . The husband and the father may . . . Be present every day
. . . Or he may earn his salary . . . While he is far away . . . It
is not just a boy or girl . . . And mommy and her sewing . . . And
not the way their problems and . . . Their obstacles are growing
. . . It is that deep affection that . . . Will conquer space and air
. . . As long as they are still in love . . . No matter when or where
. . . It all depends upon how much . . . They think about each
other . . . And if dear daddy does adore . . . The children and
their mother.

*Reading books is a matter of both spare-time interest and how
much time you have to spare. As a youngster, I read Horatio Alger,
the Rover Boys, etc., because I had the leisure and I enjoyed them.
Now I almost never pick up a book, lest it be so good that I cannot
let go of it, and I haven't the time for any but—*

MY SELDOM BOOK

I seldom ever read a book . . . But when I pick one up . . . I
cannot put it down until . . . My lips have drained the cup . . . I
start to read a chapter and . . . I go from page to page . . . And
then I am a prisoner . . . Inside the author's cage . . . Of course
the book must be a gem . . . And one that interests me . . . The
kind that seems to have a hold . . . On time and memory . . . And
when it is that special tome . . . I take a second look . . . And
usually I keep it as . . . A sort of reference book . . . I seldom
choose a volume and . . . More seldom read it through . . . I only
wish the worth-while books . . . Were not so brief and few.

*Everyone on this earth is a philosopher, in a sense. We all have
our own ideas about life and how it should be lived. But some individuals make an intensive study of it, not alone for themselves but
more especially to help others. They minister to our mental ills, and
they well deserve their—*

P H . D .

A study of the way we live . . . Creates a Ph.D. . . . And marks
another doctor of . . . Profound philosophy . . . He knows the ills
of human life . . . And how to treat each one . . . According to
our prospects and . . . Whatever we have done . . . He tells us
what we ought to do . . . And what we better not . . . To make
more money and to have . . . More coffee in our pot . . . Of
course he has opinions and . . . At times they may be wrong . . .
But generally his good advice . . . Will help us get along . . . And
when he lifts the human heart . . . That is depressed and blue . . .
He does a service on this earth . . . That very few can do.

*Loneliness is not aloneness, and you need not be alone to be lonely.
You may be all by yourself and never feel lonely, and you may be
part of a crowd—in public or at a private party—and still be utterly
alone. But when you are deeply in love, no matter where you are,
your heart is lonely when you think of your only one and you whisper: Dear, there was—*

NO WORD FROM YOU

It was a dreary day today . . . The sky was barely blue . . . And
I was lonely, dear, because . . . I did not hear from you . . . The
mailman brought no letter, love . . . The telephone was still . . .
And there were only empty hopes . . . No promise could fulfill
. . . Perhaps you were too busy or . . . Perhaps you were not well
. . . Or maybe there is some excuse . . . You do not want to tell
. . . Believe me, dear, I trust you and . . . My heart would never
doubt . . . And there is no one else on earth . . . I care to think
about . . . But, oh, today was dreary and . . . Tonight is lonely
I love you more than I can say . . . Please, let me hear

The high-pressure, fast-talking salesman may do a slick job for a while, but eventually he will have dissatisfied customers, and he will find it harder to convince new prospects. Wise is he who waits to answer questions, instead of answering them before they are asked; who lets the customer make up his own mind. He is the successful—

SILENT SALESMEN

The silent salesman is the one . . . Who almost never fails . . . And more than often is the one . . . Who makes the greatest sales . . . The silent salesman is the one . . . Who does not rant and shout . . . But who will let your mind decide . . . When there is any doubt . . . Who does not try to conquer you . . . With words a mile a minute . . . But gives you time to weigh the deal . . . and see the profit in it . . . He gives a friendly greeting, yet . . . His selling words are few . . . And there are intermissions when . . . He leaves it up to you . . . He speaks each sentence slowly and . . . He lets each word sink in . . . And by his silence in between . . . He usually will win.

It takes both a tongue and an ear to create gossip. Gossip can be vicious and most unjust. We denounce it, and yet many times we are party to it, whether on the sending or receiving end. If only we would close our ears, there could be no gossip. So—

WHY DO WE LISTEN?

Why do we ever listen to . . . The rumors that we hear . . . When just the smallest inquiry . . . May prove them insincere? . . . Why do we swallow gossip as . . . The very gospel truth . . . Without a certain knowledge of . . . Our grownups and our youth? . . . The reason is that people are . . . More ready to condemn . . . Than try to understand the ones . . . Who want to work with them . . . We are prepared to criticize . . . Reluctant to forgive . . . And we ignore our own mistakes . . . As swiftly as we live . . . So why not slow our pace a bit . . . And take another glance? . . . It may be we instead of they . . . Who need another chance.

Now it is noon. It is the noon of that day we talked about a while back in this book, in January and April. In terms of a day the year is going into its afternoon. Soon it will be evening, with time swiftly running out. Where are we? What have we done? Have we accomplished something, or don't we care—

AFTER YEAR'S NOON

One half is gone, one half remains . . . It is the year's divide . . . With chances lost and those still left . . . Upon the other side . . . Six months of days have disappeared . . . With every sun and moon . . . And now the passing of the year . . . Has reached its afternoon . . . What is our score upon the board? . . . Where do we stand today? . . . And if we lag, what true defense . . . Is there for us to say? . . . The year is going swiftly and . . . There is no time to wait . . . A few more weeks that turn to months . . . And it may be too late . . . How much have we been true to God . . . And filled our place on earth? . . . Just six more months remain for us . . . To really prove our worth.

There are those occasions when you have to be careful of talking to a stranger, but there are times when a formal introduction is not necessary. It depends on circumstances, and when the circumstances are right, there is no easier way to make friends. It is then you discover that you live in a—

FRIENDLY WORLD

Where do I find the friends I have? . . . On buses, trains and planes . . . I meet them in the sunshine and . . . I greet them in the rain . . . Around the happy neighborhood . . . In theater or store . . . Where they are seeking just as much . . . What I am looking for . . . I make my friends along the streets . . . Of cities far away . . . And it is just as pleasant there . . . To pass the time of day . . . A lake resort, a little farm . . . Wherever I may be . . . I offer them my friendly hand . . . And they give theirs to me . . . And so it seems the whole wide world . . . Down to its smallest part . . . Is hungry for the friendliness . . . Of every human heart.

December, 1963

THE HANDLEY-ADAMS AGENCY
magazine

Published as a special service to our friends and as a reminder that a professionally planned insurance program is the safer way to protect your possessions.

HINTS...

for homemakers

CANDLE HOLDERS that you make yourself can be quite elegant. For example, you can transform an empty syrup bottle into a handsome holder by decorating the bottleneck and taper with a bright ribbon bow, wired Christmas balls, and a small spray of branches.

AFTER A PARTY your living room may be all "smoked up". To banish the stale tobacco odors, add a tablespoon of ammonia to a bowl of water and place in the room after your guests leave.

TO CLEAN SILVER place a sheet of aluminum foil in an enamel or stainless steel pan. Pour in one gallon of hot water, add two ounces of good detergent. Place silver in solution. Make sure pieces touch aluminum. When stains disappear, rinse, wipe dry and store in dry place with piece of camphor. Keep silver away from rubber. Rubber tarnishes silver.

GIFT WRAPPINGS and paper ribbon can be used again. Just wipe the wrinkles and creases with a damp sponge on the back side; then iron.

small talk...

■ Here's a statistic which may be slightly discomforting: the richest man in the world has a *weekly* income of $7,280,000. This modern Croesus is His Highness Sir Abdullah al-Subah, Sultan of the tiny oil-rich kingdom of Kuwait.

■ This time of year you're apt to find that too many people are drinking on an empty head.

■ Perhaps you will not be surprised by the fact that Americans will spend more than $7 billion for Christmas gifts this year. That's a little more than we spend during the whole year for *all* birthdays, weddings, anniversaries, baby births and showers *combined!*

■ The older generation thought nothing of going to bed at 9 p.m. The younger generation doesn't think much of it either.

■ A husband who asks his wife's opinion on anything just hasn't been paying attention.

■ In case you've been wondering, the longest log-rolling contest on record took place in Chequamegon Bay, Ashland, Wisconsin in 1900 when Allen Stewart dislodged Joe Oliver from a 24-inch diameter log after three hours and 15 minutes of birling. Now you know!

The Art of Christmas Through the Ages

13th Century Master, Giotto,
"Flight into Egypt"

20th Century Artist, George
Hitchcock's, "Flight into Egypt"

THE STORY OF CHRISTMAS has inspired the world's most brilliant artists through the ages. The beauty of the story never changes, but artistic interpretations vary greatly with time and place.

A Christmas theme which has been rendered with considerable frequency through the centuries is "The Flight Into Egypt." According to Mr. Edward Oestreicher, of Oestreicher's Print Shop in New York City, there are no less than forty-nine different recorded interpretations of "Flight Into Egypt."

Among the most frequently requested reproductions is the version by the 13th Century master, Giotto, and the one by the 20th Century artist, George Hitchcock. When contrasted, the two works provide an interesting example of how interpretations of Christmas subjects change with the times.

The theme is the flight of the Holy Family from Judea after an Angel appeared to Joseph in a dream and said, "Arise, and take the young child and his mother and flee . . . "

In the Giotto painting, facial expressions help to relate the mood. Jesus appears as a happy child, while Mary seems to be brooding over the life which lies ahead of the Infant. There is sharp color contrast, a pronounced distinction between people and landscape, and a celestial feeling about the entire scene.

George Hitchcock's "Flight Into Egypt," painted 600 years later, is more realistic. It has been described as "earthy." The Mother and Child are set in a relaxed atmosphere, facial expressions are barely visible, and the whole composition seems to blend into one quiet mood.

Regardless of the school or period of painting you prefer, regardless of the master or picture which appeals to you, there is no doubt that the Christmas season is profoundly enriched by these inspired and inspirational works.

A PHILOSOPHY OF LOVE

WHEN A FATHER, so beset with emotional problems of his own that he can't think of the needs of his children, loses his job two weeks before Christmas, where does his wife turn for help? When a man, after twenty-three homeless years, finally conquers his alcoholic problem and wants to see his family again, who will help him? When a hospitalized child cries at night for a doll of her own, who will provide it?

These pleas, and many others, are heard and answered by The Salvation Army each year at Christmas time. During the holiday season, the Army provides festivities for men and women in uniform, plans parties for those without friends and families, visits the lonely aged, serves hot dinners to the homeless, and

When one's family is far away, a gift and a friendly visit from a Salvationist brighten the long, lonely hours.

brings gifts and the warmth of friendship into cold prison cells.

This tradition of sharing Christmas with others is a basic tenet of The Salvation Army. Each December thousands of dedicated Salvationists work to illumine the dark corners of life with the bright lights of faith and hope. But The Salvation Army is more than a "once-a-year" friend.

Salvationists maintain places of worship, clinics, general hospitals, maternity homes for unmarried mothers, children's homes and foster care service, settlements and day nurseries, emergency lodges for women and children, centers for transient and homeless men, correctional service bureaus for aiding prisoners and their families, bureaus for locating missing friends and relatives, employment services, boys' clubs, summer camps, Red Shield and Salvation Army-USO centers for members of the armed forces, emergency disaster shelters, services to the aging, rehabilitation centers for alcoholics, and similar allied services.

From its neighborly beginnings ("those with little helping those with less") The Salvation Army today keeps pace with the changing times. In cities, where it is

OUR COVER: The joys of Christmas can have a homey look as these two Salvation Army lassies, making home visits in the 1920's, demonstrate.

difficult to know your neighbor, much less his needs, The Salvation Army is working to bring comfort to the less fortunate.

Why has this unique Army dedicated itself to providing for the spiritual and physical needs of others? The founder of The Salvation Army, General William Booth, summed up the philosophy of love that motivates the Army when, at the turn of the century, he drafted a special message of encouragement to Salvationists throughout the world.

The longer his cablegram grew, the more General Booth thought of the expense of sending it and how the money could be used instead to feed and shelter the needy. After struggling to encompass the compassion, aims and ideals of the members of The Salvation Army in a short phrase, he finally chose one word. The word he cabled was: "Others".

Sharing with others, and especially at Christmas time, is a basic tenet of The Salvation Army. Hot holiday dinners are traditional.

Parties as well as presents for boys and girls are among the many Christmas activities of The Salvation Army.

BACK TROUBLE

The recent college students' fad for stuffing telephone booths has a counterpart in northern India. At the Pushkar Fair in the state of Rajasthan, as many Indians as possible cling to a camel's back. The idea is to test how many passengers the camel will accept and still rise to his feet. Some camels will take aboard a dozen riders.

MISS FIFI OF 1964

In Barnham, England, the organizers of an annual beauty contest recently announced that henceforth they would judge dogs instead of girls. Mrs. Alice Heritage, chairman of the annual competition, explained that Barnham lasses were all lovely, but they simply will not come forward and enter the contest. So now the same cup previously awarded to human beauty queens will be won by some canine charmer. And there is no discrimination. Dogs of both sexes may compete!

As part of our agency's P.S. (Personal Service) we are pleased to present a few insurance tips to help you save money.

LOW-COST LIFE INSURANCE

We are pleased to announce a brand new and convenient way to get life insurance, at low cost. It's called Ætna Homeowners Life, and it's available to most families who insure their homes with an Ætna Casualty Homeowners Policy. Homeowners Life is easy to buy; no medical exam required, no red tape. The policy provides a monthly income to meet individual needs, such as mortgage payments. The cost? Only $60 a year. Call for details.

STOLEN PROPERTY

A policyholder asks: "If a camera is stolen from my car, will my auto policy cover the loss?" Answer: No, it will not. Only equipment attached to your car, and the car itself, is insured against theft. You would be reimbursed if your car radio were taken but not if your portable radio were stolen. We do, however, have policies that provide this protection. Call us.

SPEEDCLAIM

The companies we represent are constantly developing new techniques to improve claim service. For example, Ætna Casualty's *Speedclaim*, provided free to auto insurance policyholders, carries the information necessary to begin the settlement of your claim immediately. With this in your car, you can often get your check right on the spot.

ON THE LIGHTER SIDE

"Mrs. Jones, can I go in your back yard and get my arrow?"

"Certainly, Johnnie, where is it?"

"I think it's stuck in your cat."

■ Smith was sitting down to breakfast one morning when he was astounded to see an announcement of his death in the newspapers.

He rushed to the phone at once to call up his boss.

"Hello," he shouted, "Did you see the announcement of my death in the newspapers?"

"Yes," the boss replied. "Where are you calling from?"

■ It was an ordinary home without a maid and seldom a guest. Therefore when dad appeared with two dinner guests from the office, the young son was anxious to help his mother.

When dinner was nearly over, the boy went to the kitchen and proudly carried in the first piece of apple pie, giving it to his father, who passed it to a guest.

The boy came in with a second piece of pie and gave it to his father who again gave it to a guest.

This was too much for the boy, who said; "It's no use, Dad. The pieces are all the same size."

■ Teenager: "Not only has he broken my heart and wrecked my life, but he's messed up my whole evening."

"What's George going as?"

The fourth grade boy who was to play the innkeeper in the school's Christmas pageant came from a very hospitable family and, since he had never seen anyone rudely turned away from his home, he burst into tears every time he had to tell Mary and Joseph there was no room in the inn. Finally, after repeated explanations that the innkeeper wasn't really unkind, that there really *wasn't* any room in the inn, the teacher thought that the little fellow understood.

The day of the pageant the school assembly hall was packed with parents. The curtain went up on Mary and Joseph standing outside the inn door. They knocked and the door was opened by a small innkeeper who said in a half-sobbing voice: "I'm sorry, but there's no room in the inn." But then, in a last desperate attempt at hospitality, he asked: "But won't you come in and have a drink?"

HANDLEY-ADAMS, INC.
1848 East Sunshine
Springfield, Mo.

(Return Requested)

Etson E. Jackson
2851 E. Crestview
Springfield, Mo.

Season's Greetings

As we approach the end of another calendar year, we welcome the opportunity to express once again our appreciation for the privilege of serving you. To you and yours—from all of us—we extend a sincere wish that the blessings of good health, good friends and good fortune may be yours in this happy holiday season and through all of the new year.

HANDLEY-ADAMS, INC.

Insurance Counsellors

1848 East Sunshine   Springfield, Mo.

Phone: TU 1-5455

Why are we so impulsive, so eager to grab our fun and happiness when holidays roll around? Why do we throw all caution to the wind? We make every effort to stay alive when we have to report for work, and yet when it comes to the time we enjoy the most—that extra day off—we ignore everything else. We forget to—

TAKE IT EASY

May you enjoy your outing on . . . The fourth day of July . . . And may it not become the day . . . Or evening that you die . . . You know, there are those crowded roads . . . With traffic everywhere . . . And all the crazy motorists . . . Who do not seem to care . . . And there are lakes and swimming pools . . . Where people could be drowned . . . And fireworks more dangerous . . . Than their explosive sound . . . There are so many accidents . . . About this time of year . . . So take it slow and easy and . . . Be sure the path is clear . . . Be mindful of your family . . . Along your merry way . . . And let no tragedy occur . . . This Independence Day.

When our forefathers declared their independence, they were concerned solely with human and personal liberty. They had no ambition to conquer and rule the world. Today our United States is a world power, but our principles and doctrines remain the same. We want democracy, human liberty and equality—

WE JUST WANT PEACE

There may not be much liberty . . . Around the world today . . . But always by the grace of God . . . We have the U.S.A. . . . And while the Stars and Stripes still fly . . . All peoples may be sure . . . That justice, truth, equality . . . And freedom will endure . . . As long as we have wisdom and . . . We know that we are right . . . And we continue to maintain . . . Our military might . . . We do not want to rule the world . . . With all its fertile sod . . . We only strive to conquer souls . . . And bring them back to God . . . We hope with all our hearts that we . . . Shall live to see the day . . . When peace will flourish everywhere . . . As in our U.S.A.

No one can "pass the buck" more effectively than Mommy. Mommy is economy-minded, and Daddy likes to be generous. When our daughter wants something, I try to get out of it, but I am just wasting my breath when I say—

GO ASK YOUR MOTHER

When darling Krissie comes to me . . . For one thing or another . . . I usually suggest that she . . . Prevail upon her mother . . . And so she skips and scampers off . . . To look for Mommy dear . . . And I relax and once again . . . My thoughts are calm and clear . . . But mine is not the happy lot . . . Of comfort unmolested . . . Where now once more my patience and . . . My nerves are being tested . . . For she comes running back to me . . . As daughters often do . . . And she reports, "Well, Mommy says . . . That it is up to you" . . . If I say no, then I become . . . A criminal to Krissie . . . If I say yes, my wife declares . . . I am a weak-kneed sissy.

"A penny for your thoughts." It is just a casual expression when two people get together and one of them is unusually silent. But how much would you really give to know someone's thoughts, especially if that someone were the one you loved? You would, no doubt, offer more than a penny in asking: What are—

YOUR THOUGHTS

A penny for your thoughts, my dear? . . . No, that would never do . . . For I would give a great deal more . . . To know that part of you . . . And I would give you everything . . . And all I am to be . . . If only now your loving thoughts . . . Were those you thought of me . . . Because I love you and because . . . Each picture in my mind . . . Is one of you—how dear you are . . . How gentle, good and kind . . . My only thoughts are those of you . . . The sweetest soul on earth . . . And being mine, they may not be . . . Of any special worth . . . But yours would ransom any king . . . Whatever they might be . . . And I sincerely hope and pray . . . They are your thoughts of me.

What does it matter if our hair becomes gray, gradually or all at once? Is there any reason to be ashamed of growing old or being gray prematurely? God gave us our hair, and if the color changes, it is by His will, and we have no cause to complain. When that time comes, let us resign ourselves to—

GRAY HAIR

Why are we so concerned about . . . A little graying hair? . . . Why do we try to pluck it out . . . Or change the color there? . . . Why do we hold the mirror and . . . Investigate our head? . . . Why does a single fiber gray . . . Induce such fear and dread? . . . We cannot change the course of time . . . The years must come and go . . . And nature has a way with us . . . The older that we grow . . . And God created nature as . . . His government on earth . . . So everyone and everything . . . Are natural from birth . . . Then let us not be so concerned . . . With pride and vanity . . . But trust in God and let our hair . . . Grow older gracefully.

No human being is able to determine the length of his or her life. We cannot be sure of living even a fraction of one more second. Why, then, take a chance on the time we have left on earth? Why delay our resignation to the will of God? Yes, we may live for many years but, then again, we may breathe—

ONLY TODAY

You do not live for 60 years . . . Of labor and of play . . . Or 70 or more than that . . . But only for today . . . God only knows how long your life . . . Will be upon this earth . . . And it is up to you to prove . . . Your everlasting worth . . . The past is gone forever and . . . Tomorrow is not here . . . And so today is all that counts . . . To prove yourself sincere . . . This day and only this one counts . . . With all the deeds you do . . . Remember that, and live for God . . . With all the soul in you . . . Remember His commandments and . . . Be everybody's friend . . . Today may be the last on earth . . . That you will ever spend.

Concealing our feelings is sometimes the best and noblest thing we can do. There are times when we feel hurt, angry or jealous, but just a bit of diplomacy can save strife, bitterness and open warfare. It might even lead to lifelong friendship, and it doesn't cost anything to—

BE POLITE

We may not always like it and . . . We may not think it right . . . But it is so much easier . . . To try to be polite . . . And it is so much happier . . . For everyone concerned . . . To have the friendly feeling that . . . No bridges have been burned . . . Of course we have our grudges and . . . Perhaps our pride is hurt . . . And maybe there were comments that . . . Were critical or curt . . . But when we get together, we . . . Should strive to put away . . . The anger and the jealousy . . . We harbored yesterday . . . And even if we feel we are . . . Completely in the right . . . At least our common decency . . . Should make us be polite.

You are so anxious to hear from someone—someone who means so much to you. At last you get a letter. It isn't the message you had hoped to get. There is no commitment, no word of affection, and yet you are grateful for those lines written in a certain hand, as you reply—

AT LEAST YOU WROTE

I thank you for your letter and . . . For every line thereof . . . I thank you for it even though . . . It never mentioned love . . . I tried to read between the lines . . . But there was nothing there . . . To say how little or how much . . . Or if at all you care . . . And yet you cared enough to write . . . If just a line or two . . . And write the precious signature . . . That is a part of you . . . I analyzed the envelope . . . And looked beneath the stamp . . . But there was nothing to behold . . . By eye or X-ray lamp . . . And yet I thank you for your words . . . And thank you lovingly . . . Because, at least that once, you took . . . The time to think of me.

A business secretary is a necessity, but a social secretary is strictly a luxury. If you can afford one, it is just like having a stenographer, maid (or butler), business manager and guardian angel all rolled into one. Who does not wish he had a—

SOCIAL SECRETARY

The social secretary is the one . . . Who reads your private mail . . . And travels with you everywhere . . . By auto, plane or rail . . . Who answers all the phone calls and . . . Politely answers "no" . . . Unless there is some reason why . . . The dialog should flow . . . Who maybe keeps your business books . . . And secret diary . . . The guardian angel of your time . . . To give you moments free . . . Employee and companion and . . . A guide in wilderness . . . This person can promote your name . . . And save you from distress . . . But first you must be able to . . . Afford such luxury . . . Then find someone whom you can trust . . . Who serves efficiently.

Friendship is something that usually develops over a period of time, but it can happen overnight. Of course, every friendship has to prove itself, which cannot be done instantly, but we should allow an open heart for both the—

NEW FRIEND OR OLD

A friend may be the one you've known . . . Through years of work and play . . . Or one who said hello to you . . . Today or yesterday . . . A friend becomes more wonderful . . . As weeks and months go by . . . And helps so much to cheer you up . . . And brighten every sky . . . But there is one you meet tonight . . . And suddenly you feel . . . There is no friendship that could be . . . More beautiful or real . . . You get together and exchange . . . The thoughts that fill the heart . . . And every sentiment appears . . . To be a common part . . . It matters not how old or new . . . A certain friend may be . . . As long as one sincerely likes . . . To share your company.

When you write a letter, you are about to mail a part of yourself. You are putting down thoughts in black and white that you may never be able to recall. Don't write and regret. Be sure, be sincere, and—

WRITE CAREFULLY

A letter is much more than just . . . The writing that we send . . . It is another visit with . . . A relative or friend . . . It is the silent conference that . . . Concerns a business deal . . . A means of telling thoughts that we . . . Might otherwise conceal . . . It carries invitations kind . . . Good wishes or regret . . . Or brings to mind the moments that . . . The heart cannot forget . . . It helps the bashful lover to . . . Present his ardent plea . . . Or delves into affairs of state . . . That challenge destiny . . . It represents and speaks for us . . . When we cannot be there . . . And that is why we ought to write . . . With thoughtfulness and care.

Yes, there are some people who know everything, and they are only too ready and eager to impress that fiction upon us. We try to offer our opinion, but it has no place in their sphere. They know it all. They cannot be told. There is no use to argue when—

SOME PEOPLE KNOW

Some people know the answers to . . . Our problems of today . . . Regardless of how young they are . . . Or somewhat old and gray . . . They figure out our politics . . . As no one else can guess . . . And they are sure that all is right . . . Or we are in a mess . . . Our world affairs, the atom bomb . . . Are easy subjects too . . . Indeed they are the geniuses . . . And there is nothing new . . . Of course they could be wrong but then . . . How could that happen here . . . When they are so intelligent . . . And they are so sincere? . . . They are so smart in telling us . . . Our one and only choice . . . How could we be so stupid as . . . To raise our humble voice?

You may take a vacation from your daily job at the office or factory, or from your household duties, but you cannot take a vacation from God. Wherever you go, whatever you do, you belong to Him, and you should never cease to think of Him. By His grace you have your life, your health and your job, and when you get a vacation, you should—

SHARE IT WITH GOD

If you are on vacation now . . . Remember God today . . . And give a little time to Him . . . From all your fun and play . . . Remember Him and pray to Him . . . If only for your sake . . . That He may bless you and forgive . . . Your very least mistake . . . You may not know it but your God . . . Is never on vacation . . . He watches over you, your home . . . And every isle and nation . . . He follows all the world each day . . . He has no time to rest . . . Except when you invite Him as . . . Your very special guest . . . And that is when you take the time . . . To kneel before His throne . . . And in the prayers you say to Him . . . He is your Guest alone.

Darling, how much can I offer you? I give you my heart, my mind, my body, and all that I am or ever will be. All of me I lay at your feet—

ALL BUT MY SOUL

How much do I adore you, dear? . . . How much am I in love? . . . As much as I behold the moon . . . And all the stars above . . . As much as you inspire me . . . To give myself to you . . . And in that inspiration, dear . . . My heart is ever true . . . I am your own forever and . . . Forever and a day . . . However you may answer me . . . Whatever you may say . . . My heart is in your loving hands . . . While I am on this sod . . . My loving heart but not my soul . . . For that belongs to God . . . My heart is yours, I cherish you . . . I hope you reach your goal . . . I give you everything except . . . My poor immortal soul.

Neighbors can be awful, and they can be wonderful. Some are jealous, spiteful and imposing; others are courteous and generous. Everyone has to live in a neighborhood. Why not be nice to our neighbors and make life easier? As for ourselves, we are happy in our neighborhood, because we have every reason to love—

OUR NEIGHBORS

They are not called the Joneses but . . . They are the folks next door . . . And every day in every way . . . We like them more and more . . . We do not envy them their home . . . Their car or any gem . . . And ours is not the common goal . . . Of keeping up with them . . . They may have many times as much . . . Or less than we possess . . . But that does not annoy us when . . . It comes to happiness . . . We simply like them for the friends . . . Who help us on our way . . . By being nice and taking time . . . To say hello each day . . . By keeping up and furthering . . . Each civic enterprise . . . And always being ready when . . . Emergencies arise.

Indeed, "travel broadens one." You never really know the world until you see it. Geographies, films and travel folders serve their purpose, but they cannot substitute for the visual contact with other places and people. Wherever you go, you—

TRAVEL AND LEARN

They say that travel broadens one . . . And it is really true . . . And maybe that philosophy . . . Is evident to you . . . Or maybe you have stayed at home . . . And you have never known it . . . That all the world is yours to hold . . . And in a sense to own it . . . With every mile you wander, there . . . Is less that you will doubt . . . And there is ever so much more . . . That you can talk about . . . You learn how other people live . . . Their fashions and traditions . . . And why there are ambassadors . . . And other special missions . . . So do a little traveling . . . If only in your car . . . You'll be amazed when you get back . . . How smart you really are.

You may "pack up your troubles in your old kit bag," but that does not mean that a smile will solve them. A smile will go a long way toward helping you to bear your burden, but sometimes a burden is so heavy that you need something—

MORE THAN A SMILE

A smile is always welcome in . . . The home or on the street . . . But it is not enough to solve . . . The problems we must meet . . . A smile is warm and comforting . . . To every injury . . . But it is not a certain cure . . . Or perfect remedy . . . It takes much more than just a smile . . . To heal the smallest hurt . . . To soothe our pride or wash away . . . The bloodstain on a shirt . . . A smile reflects a friendship but . . . There is no friendship true . . . Unless the heart and hand are there . . . To give themselves to you . . . A smile is always welcome but . . . It takes a little more . . . To calm the raging waters and . . . To reach a quiet shore.

Loneliness may surround me at times, but it cannot conquer me. I have only to think of my many wonderful friends. If need be, I can pick up the phone or drop them a line. Each true friend is a source of comfort in time of discouragement, a lifeline in the whirlpool of sorrow. My heart is happy—

IN MY FRIENDSHIPS

My soul is never weary and . . . I never feel alone . . . Because I am reminded of . . . The friendships I have known . . . The friendships of my early youth . . . In school, at work and play . . . And all the fond companionships . . . That still are mine today . . . There is no greater treasure than . . . To know that someone cares . . . Who wishes you the best of luck . . . And helps you climb the stairs . . . A friendship that is solid and . . . Beyond the widest range . . . Of time and tide and circumstance . . . And weather that will change . . . The everlasting friendship that . . . Is real, sincere and true . . . And does not measure your success . . . Or weigh the wealth of you.

When you have offered your heart to someone, and when that offer has been accepted, there are only two questions you ever want answered. How much do you love me? How long will you be true? And the more important of these must be—

HOW MUCH, MY LOVE?

How much do you belong to me? . . . What time is ours to spend? . . . Today? Tomorrow? Sunday? or . . . Forever without end? . . . How much, my love, may I be sure . . . That we shall be together . . . Whatever fortune may befall . . . Whatever kind of weather? . . . Will you be longing for me when . . . I have to go away? . . . Will you be waiting for me when . . . My ship comes in the bay? . . . I cannot live unless I know . . . Unless you say sincerely . . . That you are mine forever and . . . That you will love me dearly . . . Give me the answer in your heart . . . And tell it faithfully . . . How long, my love? How long, how much . . . Will you belong to me?

Perhaps you have an ordinary job. There is nothing wrong in that, provided you are not qualified for something better, and provided you cannot see your way clear to qualifying yourself for something better. The important thing is that you contribute the best you can to your fellow man. Ask yourself—

WHAT WORK DO YOU?

A factory, an office job . . . What difference does it make . . . If you are living for yourself . . . And no one else's sake? . . . If you have no ambition to . . . Attain a place on earth . . . Or try to be of little more . . . Than ordinary worth? . . . You may as well be simple and . . . Go on from day to day . . . And tell your little self that it . . . Was meant to be that way . . . But if you want to help the world . . . And those who look to you . . . Then you will give the best your heart . . . Is qualified to do . . . And surely you will strive to rise . . . Above the common ranks . . . To care for those you love and give . . . Your God eternal thanks.

Are you glad to be alive? Are you thankful for being on earth, for the opportunity to work and play, to share friendships and enjoy the wonders of love? Are you happy that you are you? Have you ever told that to God? Remember, He created you, and remember to say—

THANK YOU FOR LIFE

I thank You, God, for everything . . . Along my worldly way . . . My family, my home and all . . . That I possess today . . . I thank You for each garden growth . . . For meat and fish and drink . . . The air that I may breathe, and my . . . Ability to think . . . For every moment on this earth . . . Among my human brothers . . . With daily opportunities . . . To live my life for others . . . I thank You for the sunshine and . . . The bursting cloud of rain . . . For happiness and peacefulness . . . And every hurt and pain . . . I love You and I worship You . . . My God—my only One . . . And I regret each wrongful thing . . . That I have ever done.

We can save photographs and other souvenirs, but we cannot keep youth, except in our memory. So let us fill up a treasure chest of happy times and merry music while we are young—for that autumn of life when we shall cherish more and more—

OLD DAYS AND SONGS

Old days and songs become more dear . . . The older that we grow . . . The faces and the places and . . . The dreams we used to know . . . The days when youth was in its bloom . . . The songs we learned to sing . . . These are the warm, enchanting thoughts . . . We keep remembering . . . Yes, there were moments made for tears . . . And moments of regret . . . But sadness can be sweet, with no . . . Desire to forget . . . Somehow the sun seemed brighter then . . . The nights a little longer . . . And faith and hope and courage were . . . Perhaps a little stronger . . . Somehow our youth is everything . . . That never disappears . . . Except our lamp of lovelight that . . . Has lasted through the years.

It is easy to distinguish the spendthrift from the frugal person. The former does not hesitate in making his purchase, even though sometimes he cannot afford it (he may even be showing off), while the latter is obviously slow and deliberate. It is all a—

MATTER OF SPENDING

When people pay for purchases . . . It is not hard to tell . . . If their reserve is low or if . . . Their bank account is well . . . The one who seems quite careless or . . . Has fear upon his face . . . Should strive to be conservative . . . In some expensive place . . . While he who calmly makes his choice . . . And asks about the price . . . And even after that, appears . . . To think it over twice . . . Is probably a person who . . . Is somewhat well-to-do . . . Or at the least is one whose bills . . . Are seldom overdue . . . And thus it is apparent and . . . It only takes a look . . . To tell the spendthrift from the one . . . Who guards his pocketbook.

As long as we are in love we have each other to lean upon, and there is no storm or strife that we cannot face and endure. Faith and hope can conquer all obstacles. And as our love is everlasting, so also—

OUR JOY ENDURES

My love is yours, your love is mine . . . What more is there to ask . . . To give us courage to confront . . . And conquer every task? . . . We face the world together, dear . . . In happiness and plight . . . With every fond good morning and . . . With every sweet good night . . . I smile your smiles, I cry your tears . . . As much as mine are yours . . . And in the heaven of our dreams . . . Our happiness endures . . . You gave your vow, and I gave mine . . . And neither time nor tide . . . Will wash away this picture of . . . The bridegroom and his bride . . . I thank you, dear, with all my heart . . . My promise I renew . . . As much as you are part of me . . . I am a part of you.

Among the lowly occupations in this life is that of dishwasher. He works hard for many hours, and he does not get much pay. And yet in his menial job he is protecting the health of the rich, the poor and the average guy. He is rendering an important service, but who ever thinks of the—

DISHWASHER

He washes dishes all the day . . . Or through the quiet night . . . And takes the grime from tableware . . . To keep it clean and bright . . . He mixes soap and water to . . . Restore the shining face . . . Of glass and cup and saucer in . . . That certain eating-place . . . Sometimes he has to dry them too . . . And polish them himself . . . And put them in a special slot . . . Or stack them on a shelf . . . In any case his task is hard . . . And usually his pay . . . Is barely just enough for him . . . To live from day to day . . . And yet it all depends upon . . . His prowess to excel . . . If we succumb to spreading germs . . . Or keep our stomachs well.

It is a known fact that the world could never get along without women. But that is not just a matter of procreation. They are the mothers and the guardians, and beyond that—in everything we do we need—

A WOMAN'S TOUCH

A woman's touch is so much more . . . Important in this life . . . Than anything a man can do . . . To settle any strife . . . A woman's touch can heal the sick . . . Give courage to the weak . . . And offer inspiration for . . . Whatever goal they seek . . . It is indeed a magic wand . . . Of tender love and care . . . That conquers all despondency . . . And overcomes despair . . . A woman's touch is something strange . . . Yet warm and friendly, too . . . That seems to help another soul . . . Begin its life anew . . . It is the secret of the home . . . And children in her care . . . And all the other answers to . . . Her husband's fervent prayer.

The most valuable thing I can do on this earth is to help someone else. It may be in time of tragedy, in time of less serious need, or just to be of occasional service. Whether it requires money or time or effort—

I LIKE TO DO A FAVOR

I like to do a favor for . . . A stranger or a friend . . . By phone or letter or the book . . . Or money that I lend . . . I like to be of service to . . . My every fellow man . . . With compliments, suggestions and . . . In every way I can . . . For we are all together in . . . This life that we must live . . . And we can only gain as much . . . As we ourselves would give . . . Some people think that they can steal . . . Or cheat a little bit . . . But finally they cannot win . . . Or get away with it . . . Our money and our time are all . . . That we can wisely spend . . . And so I like to use them for . . . A stranger or a friend.

Marriage is supposed to be mutual—a 50-50 proposition—but now and then your score drops below par. You have not lived up to your part of the bargain. Your spouse has done everything for you. What have you done in return? Perhaps it is time for you—

TO MAKE IT UP

I love you for your gentleness . . . And for your faith in me . . . And all the goodness that you have . . . Inspired me to be . . . I love you for the confidence . . . You willingly bestow . . . But so much more because you are . . . The sweetest one I know . . . Because you never argue and . . . You do not want to fight . . . Although in nearly every case . . . You know that you are right . . . I treasure you for every tear . . . And burden that you bear . . . And I am sorry, darling, that . . . I have not done my share . . . I ask forgiveness for my wrongs . . . And promise I will do . . . As much as possible, my love . . . To make it up to you.

*When the life of your loved one—especially your little child—
hangs on the thread of a delicate medical operation, how do you feel?
Will you take the chance, or would you rather wait and see what
happens? Why not let science try, and leave the rest—*

AS GOD DECIDES

When there is need for surgery . . . And heavy hangs the knife
. . . Sometimes the doctor is in doubt . . . That it will save a life
. . . And sometimes patients feel the same . . . Or parents will
declare . . . That they prefer to leave it in . . . The hands of luck
or prayer . . . But when an operation seems . . . The only remedy
. . . We ought to put our trust in God . . . With all simplicity . . .
We ought to take that final chance . . . And leave it up to God
. . . If one more body that He made . . . Should stay upon this
sod . . . So let the surgery reveal . . . That God has called His
kind . . . Or else the body lives and He . . . Has something else
in mind.

*The cost of buying clothes, especially feminine apparel, is quite
an item, and perhaps the principal reason is the constant change in
style. But in the long run we are better off, because milady's new hat
or dress, or hubby's impressive suit and handsome shoes, lift the heart
and give a lilt to life. Give thanks for—*

MODERN FASHION

The fashion shops are filled with clothes . . . Of all the latest
styles . . . To make us more attractive and . . . To cultivate our
smiles . . . Of course we could go on and wear . . . The same
things every day . . . And if we did, we certainly . . . Would save
some cash that way . . . But it would be a weary life . . . And this
a sorry place . . . If we had nothing to improve . . . Or compli-
ment the face . . . The dressing habit means much more . . .
Than just to look real nice . . . By spending lavishly or by . . .
The luck of bargain price . . . It tends to keep our courage up . . .
With joy and hope renewed . . . And helps us through our struggles
with . . . A brighter attitude.

When you snub someone, when you turn that cold shoulder, you are holding yourself aloof, and in effect you are telling yourself that you are better than your neighbor. Are you? Who are you to judge? You could be wrong. Then—

WHY SO COLD?

Why must there be receptions cold . . . Beneath whatever roof? . . . The humble home or palace great . . . Where people are aloof? . . . Why must we set our friendship scales . . . According to a price . . . Instead of by the weight of souls . . . Their virtue and their vice? . . . It matters not how much we have . . . Or what we hope to gain . . . Or whether there is sunshine or . . . The day belongs to rain . . . Why turn the shoulder that is cold . . . Or freeze the smallest smile . . . When happiness and sympathy . . . Are so much more worth while? . . . The only thing that matters from . . . Beginning to the end . . . Is just that someone longs to be . . . Our true and loving friend.

The clock is important and sometimes indispensable to work. But I have often wondered about the time clock, the one where you punch a card on your way in and out. It records how long you were there, but it cannot show how hard you worked or how much you produced. Results are all that really count when it comes to—

CLOCK VS. WORK

I know a boss who does not scold . . . The ones who come in late . . . If they perform their office work . . . And keep it up to date . . . And they may take an extra while . . . When they are out to lunch . . . Without the slightest reprimand . . . Or any clock to punch . . . It is the sort of system that . . . No person can abuse . . . Because results control the job . . . That he will keep or lose . . . And if employees get behind . . . They still can save the day . . . By catching up through overtime . . . Without some added pay . . . It seems to me much better than . . . The checking in and out . . . Of those who may be prompt but whose . . . Production we may doubt.

*Yes, August is romantic, and more than one "summer love affair"
begins to blossom during this month. But true love is not born of the
warm breath of moon and stars, nor does it die in the cold wind of
snow and sleet. Every girl should be sure he is sincere when he says:
I love—*

YOU IN AUGUST

August is romantic with . . . Its flowers and its skies . . . Sunny
days and starry nights . . . Soft and lovely eyes . . . Eyes that are
the same as yours . . . When you look at me . . . Every time I
have the chance . . . To share your company . . . Is it August?—
no, I know . . . It's because of you . . . I am yours, my darling,
and . . . I promise to be true . . . All the flowers and the skies
. . . Make no difference, dear . . . I am not concerned about . . .
The season of the year . . . But August always seems to be . . . A
sort of magic way . . . And so again I promise you . . . My loving
heart today.

August 5

*There is one word in the dictionary more vague than most others.
It is a sort of catchall for everything that is left over and that does
not mean anything in particular. It is that which cannot be classified
or identified exactly. It is merely—*

MISCELLANEOUS

There is a word we often use . . . That seems to save some fuss
. . . The easy and the simple term . . . Of "miscellaneous" . . .
We use it in the office and . . . Our family budget too . . . To
cover up the extra cost . . . Of what we want to do . . . There is
a "miscellaneous" . . . For something extra spent . . . Beyond the
daily groceries . . . And paying up the rent . . . But sometimes
there are questions and . . . A sudden burst of rain . . . And
"miscellaneous" is not . . . So easy to explain . . . Of course it can
be proper but . . . It also can conceal . . . The items miscellaneous
. . . That are not really real.

Do you doubt or deny that there is a God? If you do, what have you got to gain—worldly wealth, pleasure, comfort? How long will they last? You know, you have to die—all creatures die. Death may be the end of you, but just suppose there is a God, and you are wrong—

WHY NOT BELIEVE?

Do you believe in God? Do you . . . Believe in Judgment Day? . . . Do you believe that by His will . . . The world will pass away? . . . Or do you think that you will die . . . And you will be no more . . . And nothing will be left of you . . . Except your earthly score? . . . Remember that you have a mind . . . With which you may decide . . . Remember that your will is free . . . To follow either tide . . . But die you must, and no one knows . . . What will become of you . . . And there is no assurance that . . . Your life will start anew . . . Your mind may doubt there is a God . . . You have the chance to choose . . . But if you do believe in Him . . . What have you got to lose?

The sun is a digger of graves. Every time it goes down it buries our mistakes, our heartaches, and our sorrows. Some tragedies may linger through the dawn, yet when the sun appears again, it draws our hearts to God, and it brings new hope, as He offers us—

ANOTHER CHANCE

We have regrets and sorrows as . . . We go along our way . . . But when the day is over, they . . . Belong to yesterday . . . We have to put them out of mind . . . And start this life anew . . . With faith and courage, hope and love . . . In everything we do . . . We cannot cling to tragedy . . . Or worry over strife . . . If ever we expect to be . . . Of usefulness in life . . . We have to overlook the past . . . And try to look ahead . . . For what is over now is gone . . . And what is gone is dead . . . The sun is in the heavens and . . . The sky is clear and blue . . . And we still have another chance . . . To make our dreams come true.

Friends taken lightly are friends soon forgotten. We meet them today, forget them tomorrow. They could become the best friends we ever had, if only we would try to cultivate their affection by keeping in touch with them. It does not require much effort. Just a little thoughtfulness will help us to—

HOLD ON TO FRIENDS

A friendship is a precious thing . . . And yet there comes a day . . . When somehow, unexpectedly . . . It seems to slip away . . . It is not any sudden turn . . . That changes everything . . . But just like winter walks away . . . And blends into the spring . . . It is a process natural . . . And gradual as life . . . It simply disappears without . . . A memory or strife . . . It happens to a lot of friends . . . It could be said of you . . . Unless your friendship with your friends . . . Is always tried and true . . . Don't let it happen to yourself . . . Keep every friend you know . . . Your friendships pave the pleasant path . . . Wherever you may go.

He is not a spy and, now that he has to be registered, he is not an undercover agent in the common sense, but he is there at the side of Congress to use the influence of his superiors in behalf of or against possible legislation. He is the—

LOBBYIST

The lobbyist is more or less . . . A special interest minion . . . Whose purpose is to influence . . . Political opinion . . . He lives in Washington and spends . . . His time upon the Hill . . . With ears for rumors and an eye . . . On every pending bill . . . To keep his bosses well informed . . . On House and Senate clashes . . . And see that no curtailing act . . . Or regulation passes . . . It may be for a union or . . . A corporation huge . . . In any case, he really is . . . A special sort of stooge . . . And as he struggles to promote . . . Each profitable measure . . . His reputation and his job . . . Are not exactly pleasure.

August 10

Only you can know if you are in love. You cannot be sure that your partner is in love with you, except as he or she tells you. So there is nothing wrong in asking this all-important question—

ARE WE IN LOVE?

Are you in love with me, or is . . . My heart in love with you?
. . . Or is it really mutual . . . With happiness for two? . . . I
wonder if you dream of me . . . When twilight turns to dawn . . .
When there is purple in the sky . . . And all the stars are gone
. . . I wonder if you think of me . . . When I am far away . . .
Or if your every joy in life . . . Depends upon today . . . I can
provide the answer to . . . One simple question, dear . . . I love
you and I cherish you . . . And I am so sincere . . . The other
answer is your own . . . Whatever it may be . . . Are you uncertain, darling, or . . . Are you in love with me?

August 11

It is a common habit to be careless about our obligations. Let's put them off until tomorrow—we have more important things to do today. Or do we? The longer we delay our duties and our promises, the more difficult it becomes to fulfill them. Why not be faithful as we go along? Why not pay—

OUR DEBT TODAY

We walk around the calendar . . . Along our daily way . . .
And nothing seems to matter much . . . Except the time of day
. . . We have appointments by the clock . . . At 9 or 12 or 3 . . .
Who cares about tomorrow or . . . About eternity? . . . The only
thing that matters is . . . That special luncheon date . . . Or some
inviting party that . . . May run a little late . . . Tomorrow is a
long way off . . . The bills can be delayed . . . And somehow in
the course of time . . . Our debts will all be paid . . . But what
if some tomorrow comes . . . With obligations clear . . . And we
are out of money or . . . We are not even here?

The family budget, I have learned, is a necessary evil, but not in the usual sense of that term. It is a necessary evil because it is designed to avoid the evil of spending without planning, and in order to keep it properly it is necessary to have a good—

BUDGET BOSS

My wife kept up the budget book . . . For many years and more . . . But now it is my problem when . . . We walk into a store . . . She made the budget all my own . . . As pretty as you please . . . Because I sort of criticized . . . Or I would like to tease . . . And now I must confess I have . . . A problem on my hands . . . With all the things we need and all . . . The family demands . . . I did not know how hard she worked . . . And how she tried to save . . . Until I tried the budget book . . . And I became its slave . . . And now I must apologize . . . For all the brains I lack . . . And humbly hope and pray that she . . . Will take the budget back.

"Everything comes to him who waits." Take your time. Be patient. We have heard these admonitions time and again, but everyone is in a hurry. Everyone wants to win and get rich today. How many fall by the wayside? How many lose a fortune as quickly as they make it? How many never even make it? Let us say a—

PRAYER FOR PATIENCE

Sometimes I am impatient, God . . . I do not want to wait . . . To gain a special goal in life . . . Or meet a certain date . . . Sometimes I am impetuous . . . And now and then I fret . . . Because I have not gotten all . . . The things I want to get . . . And so today I ask You for . . . The patience that I need . . . To cope with every hope I have . . . And every wishful deed . . . Please teach me, God, to take my time . . . And let the days fulfill . . . My fondest dreams according to . . . Your good and holy will . . . Give me the patience to go on . . . Through struggle and through strife . . . And in my poor and humble way . . . To persevere in life.

Soldiers, Boy Scouts and little children still use tents. The circus has to have them, and sailboats could not navigate without that special canvas that billows on the wind-swept sea. We thank the ones who make our—

SAILS AND TENTS

It takes an expert hand to make . . . That covering for others . . . The sturdy sails for yachtsmen true . . . Or tents for Ringling Brothers . . . Designs are cut and ropes are spliced . . . And sewed with needle blunt . . . And there must be sufficient slack . . . For every tack or stunt . . . The needle must not pierce the rope . . . That forms the solid binding . . . But it must move between the strands . . . According to their winding . . . Together at the circus or . . . Adrift upon the sea . . . Our hearts are grateful to the hands . . . That sew so expertly . . . It is a craft that comes to us . . . From many canvas tailors . . . Especially the ones who served . . . The old Norwegian sailors.

It is one thing to propose marriage, quite another to be accepted. You think that you are quite a prize for the one you have chosen. You finally admit you have fallen in love, but in the last analysis it occurs to you that you must say—

I HOPE YOU WILL

I may as well admit it, dear . . . I am in love with you . . . When I am feeling wonderful . . . Or I am feeling blue . . . When everything is beautiful . . . With sunshine everywhere . . . Or when the rain is rushing down . . . And no one seems to care . . . Whatever mood or weather, dear . . . The answer is the same . . . I only see your friendly face . . . I only hear your name . . . You are forever in my mind . . . No matter where I go . . . And in my loving heart you are . . . The only one I know . . . What more is there to offer you? . . . What else is there to say? . . . I hope you feel the same and you . . . Will set the wedding day.

When friends get together for a visit, there is nothing like a cup of steaming coffee or a brace of hot tea. It seems to add flavor to the conversation, and in that pleasant atmosphere we enjoy more the aroma from—

THE FRIENDLY CUP

I always like to have my friends . . . With coffee or with tea . . . It seems the beverage adds a zest . . . To their good company . . . We pour a cup with sugar spiced . . . Some lemon juice or cream . . . And then we sit and talk of life . . . And meditate and dream . . . A sweet aroma fills the air . . . From foreign bean or leaf . . . And as the clock is shaking hands . . . The time is all too brief . . . The hour of the day or night . . . Is not important then . . . Because we never know for sure . . . When we shall meet again . . . But now the coffee or the tea . . . Is warm and good inside . . . And for this moment in the best . . . Of friendship we abide.

August has always moved me as the month of dreams and memories. It is the time when I like to review my mental diary of the summer that is drawing to a close, and of all the summers and years that have gone before. Yes, I like to dream—

IN AUGUST

In August there is time to dream . . . And count the days gone by . . . To smell the pretty flowers and . . . To walk around and sigh . . . To ponder all the memories . . . That paved the passing miles . . . With tears and disappointments and . . . Success and sunny smiles . . . In August there are hopes and schemes . . . That open every door . . . To all the secret treasures and . . . The ships that come ashore . . . It is the time for happiness . . . If only for a day . . . Before the blooms of summer fade . . . And petals fall away . . . Before the autumn comes along . . . To overpaint the trees . . . With colors bright that magnify . . . The new-born memories.

Today is the birthday of our darling daughter, Kristina Maria. Of course, I also love our two handsome sons, Jimmie and Don, but there is something about a girl—well, as I have always said, "Boys are nice but girls are sweet." One thing especially sweet about Krissie is that she is so much like her Mommy. Kristina's age? It doesn't matter. She will always be—

MY LITTLE GIRL

My little girl is wonderful . . . And sweet as she can be . . . What other words of love and praise . . . Could you expect from me? . . . She is my young Kristina and . . . The dearest girl on earth . . . And I have always loved her from . . . The moment of her birth . . . And now that she is growing up . . . More lovely every day . . . She looks and acts like Mommy dear . . . In every happy way . . . She is the image of the girl . . . Who once became my wife . . . And who is mine to have and hold . . . Forever in this life . . . Kristina is my Lillian . . . And still my darling Kris . . . And both of them belong to me . . . In every hug and kiss.

There is quite some difference between a vacation junket and traveling on business. You may feel relaxed in the confidence of your ability, but you have to dress up and keep on your toes when you go on a—

BUSINESS TRIP

Your travels on vacation days . . . Are filled with joy and fun . . . But not the trips you take alone . . . To get your business done . . . For then you must arrive on time . . . At some specific spot . . . And there are notes and mental plans . . . That dare not be forgot . . . You have to keep appointments at . . . The second they are fixed . . . And let no business data or . . . A name or face get mixed . . . Your clothes must be in perfect shape . . . Your eyes and shoes must shine . . . And you should have sufficient cash . . . Wherever you may dine . . . It makes a world of difference on . . . A plane, a train or ship . . . If you are just vacationing . . . Or it's a business trip.

It is not selfish to pray for yourself alone, if you pray to live a better life, because the better you live, the more you serve your neighbor. Thus it can be your most—

IMPORTANT PRAYER

The most important prayer on earth . . . That we can ever say . . . Is that which asks the grace of God . . . To live His holy way . . . The prayer to keep our faith in Him . . . And glorify His name . . . Beyond all wealth and glory and . . . Above all worldly fame . . . To put aside our selfishness . . . Our jealousy and hate . . . And recognize the emptiness . . . Of temporal estate . . . For we are only in this life . . . According to His will . . . And clearly He has given His . . . Commandments to fulfill . . . So let us kneel and let us say . . . This most important prayer . . . To honor God above all else . . . And praise Him everywhere.

Every year there are those summer romances that seem so wonderful, only to end up in broken hearts. Usually (though not always) it is the boy who makes a pretense at love, so don't be crestfallen if your girl friend doubts your sentiments. You may have to do double duty to convince her that your love is—

NO MERE VACATION LOVE

My love is not vacation love . . . It is not just a play . . . I offer you my faithful heart . . . Forever and a day . . . The moon is not a sorcerer . . . Who has imprisoned me . . . And I am not in love with you . . . Just temporarily . . . You need not fear that our canoe . . . Will vanish in a mist . . . Or that I ever shall forget . . . That moment when we kissed . . . When summer fades to autumn, dear . . . My thoughts will be the same . . . And every letter will begin . . . With your beloved name . . . My love for you is constant as . . . The sun and stars above . . . It is not just a fancy or . . . A mere vacation love.

Life is the one outstanding thing that does not belong to us. It belongs to God. We have no right to tamper with it, and if we dare to destroy it with our own hand, we are defying God. This applies just as much to our own life as to that of another. So—

WHY SUICIDE?

Why does a man or woman take . . . The suicidal way? . . . What causes them to put an end . . . To every night and day? . . . Is living so expensive that . . . We cannot meet the cost? . . . Is everything so hopeless that . . . We seem forever lost? . . . No, these are not the answers to . . . The problems they propose . . . And life is not as difficult . . . As people may suppose . . . Success in life depends upon . . . Our willingness to give . . . As much as we can do our best . . . To help the world to live . . . And as we clench our fists, and face . . . The struggle and the strife . . . Let us remember God alone . . . Has power over life.

How careless, how thoughtless can we get? For the mere convenience of tossing away a lighted match or cigaret, or ignoring the remains of a campfire, we risk the loss of thousands of beautiful trees, as well as human and animal life. Worst offender of all is the selfish, self-important, "I-don't-care" character, who has no desire to—

PROTECT OUR FORESTS

Our land is rich in forests and . . . In parks with flowers fair . . . And many are the ones who like . . . To spend their leisure there . . . But some do not appreciate . . . The caution that is needed . . . And they will let all warnings and . . . Reminders go unheeded . . . The danger of a fire from . . . A flying spark at night . . . The cigaret, cigar or pipe . . . That still retains its light . . . It takes so little effort to . . . Prevent a conflagration . . . And save the vast resources and . . . The beauty of our nation . . . Let's be more careful when we drive . . . Or camp beneath the trees . . . To save our forests and avoid . . . The human tragedies.

As long as we have state sovereignty, the position of governor will be one of the most important in the land. Yet, by the grace of God and our democratic form of government, it will always be for the people to decide upon their own—

GOVERNOR

He is the ruler of a state . . . As much as people rule . . . As much as he is capable . . . And he has learned in school . . . He tells the legislature his . . . Opinions and his views . . . And does his best to guide them in . . . The way they think and choose . . . He may attempt to be the king . . . And run the show himself . . . And take the laws he does not like . . . And put them on the shelf . . . But when the votes are counted by . . . The pencil or machine . . . They spell the final reckoning . . . Of what the people mean . . . And first and last and always now . . . His victory will be . . . If he can gather in the votes . . . For his majority.

Treasure each friendship while you can. You never know how long it will last. Some friends move away and forget you, others gradually disappear from your daily circle. One of my dearest friends was called home by God about two years after we met. Friends linger for years or just a day. They are—

NOT ALL FOR LIFE

Some friends cannot be friends for life . . . They simply come and go . . . Although they may be extra good . . . And wonderful to know . . . They may be forced to move away . . . And through their busy year . . . They may just gradually forget . . . And slowly disappear . . . Or they may suffer illness or . . . A tragedy one day . . . Or by the will of God the heart . . . May live its final day . . . And so in every friendship new . . . Let us remember this . . . That there are some who cannot last . . . And some whom we shall miss . . . But also by the will of God . . . And by the grace He sends . . . We may enjoy the company . . . Of many lifelong friends.

We may have met our spouse in early youth, in middle age, or even late in life. However late or early, our love spans the years to the very beginning of the one we cherish. It seems that certain someone was always in our heart. In my own case I feel that is the true—

SYMBOL OF MY LOVE

If all the days and months and years . . . Of time were put together . . . And all the winds and rains and snows . . . And every kind of weather . . . And if I could have lived them all . . . And known you from the start . . . You would have been and still would be . . . The creature of my heart . . . And if my love through all that time . . . Could fit into a thimble . . . It would adorn your finger as . . . A faithful, boundless symbol . . . The real and soulful symbol of . . . How much you mean to me . . . As long as there is any life . . . And through eternity . . . Because by any mete or bound . . . As time and tide may measure . . . You are the one I always loved . . . And I shall always treasure.

How much does your church mean to you? It tries to help you find your way to God, to comfort and encourage you, and it needs your support. Its only sustenance is your charity. It makes no demands. In your heart you hold one of the only two keys to its doors—generosity or stinginess. The former will open them wide. The latter may lock them forever—to you and your neighbors—

WHAT WILL YOU GIVE?

How much will you contribute to . . . The work of God today? . . . What will be your donation when . . . The basket comes your way? . . . You know, the church depends on you . . . For what support it lacks . . . Without initiation fee . . . Or any dues or tax . . . It is your generosity . . . That helps maintain the church . . . So other souls that look for God . . . May end their weary search . . . Be generous in church today . . . As much as you can be . . . And do it with your smiling heart . . . And not begrudgingly . . . Your dollars do much more for God . . . Than they can do for you . . . And for each one His blessing will . . . Be worth much more than two.

The home has its comfort and security, but only outdoors can we really commune with nature, experience the adventure and excitement of earth in bloom, and feel closer to God. Whatever season, when the weather permits, it is good for us—

TO BE OUTDOORS

I like to walk on country lanes . . . And wander through the woods . . . And look around for animals . . . In brushy neighborhoods . . . To pick the berries that are wild . . . And pretty flowers too . . . And learn the habits of the birds . . . As nature lovers do . . . I am no ornithologist . . . Or keeper of the bees . . . But I adore the outdoor world . . . The rivers and the trees . . . The lakes where people fish all day . . . And make their camp at night . . . And sing the songs of long ago . . . Around the firelight . . . I like to leave the city with . . . Its buildings and its cars . . . And try to get a closer look . . . At God's array of stars.

One day you feel like working your head off, the next day you're in a slump. Maybe it is your fault, or maybe your job is not the right one for you. You might blame it on human nature, but you would have a hard time explaining that to the boss who thinks you should always be in the—

MOOD TO WORK

One day I do not want to work . . . Another day I do . . . And when my mind is in the mood . . . I really follow through . . . I get my duties all lined up . . . And do them one by one . . . And it is hardly any time . . . Before they all are done . . . I only wish that I could keep . . . A much more even keel . . . And do my duties day by day . . . No matter how I feel . . . It would be so much happier . . . To keep a steady pace . . . And it would put a brighter look . . . On my employer's face . . . But sometimes I am in the mood . . . And sometimes I am not . . . And that is my particular . . . And my peculiar lot.

Although I am no longer haunted by the daily deadlines of newspaper work, there are some things that cannot be put off, such as copy for syndication or the manuscript for a book. And that brings up the problem I have with my children, as now and then they get in the way of—

DADDY'S DEADLINES

When I am concentrating in . . . The confines of my study . . . My youngsters always dash right in . . . With smiles and faces ruddy . . . "Hey, Daddy, take a look at this!" . . . Or, "May I have some money?" . . . And so it goes with Jimmie, Don . . . And my Kristina honey . . . I try to make them understand . . . We have to live and eat . . . And there are deadlines in my work . . . I am compelled to meet . . . But they are never troubled by . . . The time that I must measure . . . Except as it may interfere . . . With problem or with pleasure . . . "Why must you have a deadline, Dad . . . And always be right on it? . . . Your time is never ours to share . . . When we depend upon it."

A knot is better than a "not," when it comes to love, and no one appreciates that more than a sailor. The seaman has knots to tie with rope, and knots to sail on the sea, but if he is in love, he is thinking of only one, and he is writing to her about—

OUR LOVING KNOT

Good night, my love, and may this be . . . The last time that I say . . . Good night, my love, with all my heart . . . These many miles away . . . Tomorrow as I start to sail . . . The distance will grow less . . . And every wind will cut the knots . . . Between our happiness . . . And when the ocean knots are gone . . . The only knot will be . . . The one I tied around your heart . . . To keep you close to me . . . You tied it too with loving words . . . That gave your promise true . . . And you are mine forever now . . . As I belong to you . . . Good night, my love, until the dawn . . . When all the anchors rest . . . And you and I embrace again . . . And build our little nest.

Our calendar begins in January, but the school year starts in September, and so does the social year. Vacations are about over, sleepy summer is closing its eyes for the last time, and vibrant autumn is stirring on the city street and in the country air. We yawn and stretch, jump out of bed, and race into—

HAPPY SEPTEMBER

September is that special time . . . Of hope and fantasy . . . And more than any other thing . . . Of youthful memory . . . The memory of childhood days . . . When school bells used to ring . . . Of teen-age years when flowers were . . . The proper gift to bring . . . When all that really mattered was . . . That sweet and bashful smile . . . And those dear mannerisms that . . . Were certain to beguile . . . September is a fairy from . . . The land we used to know . . . And through the dark of older years . . . Her candle seems to glow . . . September is a seldom month . . . That has but 30 days . . . But it is filled with pleasure in . . . So many lasting ways.

The most important human element in surviving a serious illness it not necessarily the skill of the doctor. More often it is our own desire to go on living. Our physician can do just so much. The rest depends on us, and sometimes our only chance for recovery is—

THE WILL TO LIVE

Whatever skill or medicine . . . The doctor tries to give . . . He cannot help the failing heart . . . That does not want to live . . . There is no knife or serum new . . . When death is at the door . . . To save the vessel that is wrecked . . . And bring it back to shore . . . It is a matter of the mind . . . And of the heart and soul . . . And that determination to . . . Attain a certain goal . . . A doctor can be famous and . . . Successful everywhere . . . But he may not be equal to . . . The symptoms of despair . . . And there is nothing he can do . . . And nothing he can give . . . Unless the patient looks to God . . . And has the will to live.

[131]

You may ask yourself, "Why do I have to pray, when God put me in this world, and He knows my troubles and my needs?" All that is true, but God did not create our troubles. He gave us a free will, and when difficulties arise, especially from our own, individual undoing, He wants us to turn to Him and ask His help. That is why—

WE HAVE TO PRAY

God knows our needs and every wish . . . We make from day to day . . . So why should we be worried now . . . And take the time to pray? . . . Whatever sorrow fills the heart . . . However trouble grows . . . Are these not all the thorns of life . . . That He already knows? . . . Yes, there is nothing ever that . . . Is hidden from His view . . . Including all our problems and . . . The trials we go through . . . But, oh, He loves to hear us plead . . . And beg Him for His aid . . . And whisper humbly that we are . . . So lonely and afraid . . . He wants to know that we believe . . . And that we lean on Him . . . And as we pray, He will not let . . . The light of hope grow dim.

Every month has its flower and birthstone, as well as its special meaning to certain individuals, and all the more if they are in love. For some it may be June or April, for others—

SEPTEMBER LOVE

I offer you the aster and . . . The morning-glory too . . . The sapphire of September, dear . . . And all my love for you . . . I give you my tomorrow and . . . My every day today . . . My heart is yours to hold, my love . . . In every special way . . . I am your own forever, dear . . . If you will be my own . . . And you will share this life with me . . . Together and alone . . . Just you and I for evermore . . . Before the fireplace . . . Without the smallest mirror to . . . Reflect your pretty face . . . I kiss you in September when . . . The flowers are so sweet . . . And then and now and always, dear . . . I worship at your feet.

Labor Day is the time we set aside each year to honor those who toil and struggle with their hands for our common welfare and our common needs. Where would we be without those hands that turn the wheels of industry and move the commerce of the world? Let us praise and give thanks—

FOR THOSE WHO LABOR

Labor Day is every day . . . If we are laboring . . . But now it is a special time . . . To celebrate and sing . . . It is the day we set aside . . . In every new September . . . For all the working hands and hearts . . . To honor and remember . . . Labor Day is not the day . . . For any clock to punch . . . Or cause to worry how we spend . . . The time we have for lunch . . . It is the time for us to give . . . Our gratitude to others . . . Who work for us and all the world . . . As laborers and brothers . . . And so we want to honor them . . . And all our praises say . . . To those for whom we set aside . . . This special Labor Day.

School days are here again, with their opportunity to learn, to mingle with classmates and form new friendships, to engage in sports and social activities, and look forward to graduation. If the school bell has stopped ringing for us, at least we have fond memories of those days when it was—

TIME FOR SCHOOL

It's time to go to school again . . . And learn a little more . . . To use when opportunity . . . Is knocking on the door . . . A little more of algebra . . . Or how to read and write . . . Philosophy or science or . . . To be a legal light . . . Vacation days are over and . . . Tuition time is here . . . As well as time for football and . . . The chance to yell and cheer . . . It means a lot of study and . . . Examinations tough . . . But there are happy moments, too . . . And life is not so rough . . . And there is youth as bright and bold . . . As ever it can be . . . With dreams that climb the ladder to . . . That coveted degree.

*It is one thing to criticize or condemn, quite another to ridicule.
"And they spat on Him . . . and kept striking Him on the head.
And when they had mocked Him . . ." That is ridicule, in the
words of St. Matthew. No one is more despicable than he—*

WHO RIDICULES

To criticize is bad enough . . . But there is no excuse . . . For
any kind of ridicule . . . That anyone lets loose . . . For ridicule
is only scorn . . . That shows a dirty sneer . . . A pattern that is
woven by . . . The threads of hate and fear . . . In any form of
ridicule . . . The Devil always thrives . . . As he attempts to un-
dermine . . . And ruin human lives . . . It is contemptible and
mean . . . To say the very least . . . And as a person ridicules
. . . His stature is decreased . . . That man or woman scarce deserves . . . The title of a fool . . . Who has the ignorance, the
grudge . . . Or spite to ridicule.

*No true friendship is determined by a sudden meeting, nor is it
cemented by a casual hello now and then. A friendship must be
proved by mutual and constant devotion. That is the only test that
matters when you ask yourself—*

WHO IS MY FRIEND?

Who is my brother in this world? . . . Who is my lasting friend?
. . . Who is the creature tried and true . . . On whom I may depend? . . . Is he the brother of my blood? . . . Is he the one I
know . . . Because we just shook hands today . . . Or many years
ago? . . . There may be other answers but . . . I think it all depends . . . Upon the character of those . . . Who want to live as
friends . . . Who really mean the words they say . . . And carry
out the creed . . . That every friend in time of need . . . Becomes
a friend indeed . . . My friend is one who thinks of me . . . As
some important guest . . . And offers all my family . . . His most
and very best.

When you fall in love and get married, there can be no parting
of the hearts; that is, if you are really in love. There will be tears and
disappointments, but one of you will give in and say to the other—

YOU MAY BE SURE

I thank you for today and for . . . The prospects of tomorrow
. . . And I am sorry, dear, if I . . . Have caused you any sorrow
. . . I only want your happiness . . . As much as it can be . . .
As much as I belong to you . . . And you belong to me . . . We
gave our promise unto God . . . That we would stay together . . .
Whatever tribulation or . . . The changing of the weather . . .
You have been wonderful to me . . . In every loving way . . . And
all my thanks are not enough . . . For what I want to say . . . But
in your heart you may be sure . . . That I shall leave you never
. . . I am your own to have and hold . . . Forever and forever.

September 10

It is difficult for human beings to be impartial in even the little
things of life. Think how much harder it must be for a judge to try
to put aside all prejudice and personal opinion when he hears or
tries a case, especially one that comes under our criminal laws. No
doubt he asks divine help, as he whispers a—

JUDGE'S PRAYER

With heart and soul I look to God . . . And say this fervent
prayer . . . That in the trial of each case . . . I may be just and
fair . . . That I may always judge the facts . . . According to the
law . . . And my decision may be right . . . Without the slightest
flaw . . . That no conviction may be wrong . . . And no defend-
ant die . . . Because of any real mistake . . . The jury made or I
. . . I pray to God that I may give . . . The judgment that is best
. . . Whatever civil wrong was done . . . Or crime that was con-
fessed . . . God only knows the sentence that . . . Befits my fellow man . . . And I depend upon His help . . . To do the best
I can.

Maybe you think the sports writer has an easy job. He gets passes to all the games, and is always assured of the best view possible. But while you are relaxing and enjoying the contest, he is analyzing it, and when you go home to rest or play, he has to pound that type-writer. It's no cinch to be a—

SPORTS WRITER

He plays when we are working, or . . . At least he takes his rest . . . But when we play by night or day . . . He must produce his best . . . His working hours are not ours . . . For his are at the game . . . And through the while we celebrate . . . The outcome we acclaim . . . In football, baseball, basketball . . . In golf or on the track . . . He strives to tell the story with . . . His special skill and knack . . . He pounds the keys from A to Z . . . To etch the picture true . . . With here and there a sideline glance . . . At records old and new . . . He seems to have a pleasant job . . . With passes at the gate . . . But few have any tougher job . . . Or ever work more late.

When summer begins we look forward to a long season of fun and pleasure. Later on it may seem to drag, and then all of a sudden it is disappearing, and we wonder where it all went. About this time we wish we could prolong—

SUMMER'S VISIT

Summer is a visitor . . . Who seems to stay and stay . . . And then before we realize it . . . Her smile has slipped away . . . When she is here the days are long . . . And bright with every pleasure . . . Although at times they seem to stretch . . . Until they're hard to measure . . . But suddenly the sun goes down . . . And stars come out too soon . . . And ever earlier the earth . . . Is greeted by the moon . . . And then we sort of stop to think . . . And maybe even worry . . . And wish our happy visitor . . . Were not in such a hurry . . . Summer is a visitor . . . We all appreciate . . . But somehow never quite enough . . . Until it is too late.

*Youth is generally free to choose its own company, good or bad,
and it is not wise for parents to interfere in the selection of friends.
However, if the child has been raised properly, the parents should
have no fear that their offspring will associate with—*

BAD COMPANY

When youngsters get themselves involved . . . In some delin-
quency . . . Their parents always shake their heads . . . And
blame bad company . . . Some youth in school or on the street . . .
Who led their son astray . . . Or taught their daughter to be "smart"
. . . And live a different way . . . But how does company begin?
. . . And who must make the choice . . . Without or with the
guiding words . . . Of some parental voice? . . . If every child
were brought up right . . . There could not ever be . . . That dev-
astating influence . . . Of evil company . . . And even in the face
of it . . . If taught the good from bad . . . No child would choose
companionship . . . It never should have had.

*Which would you rather receive—flowers or loving thoughts? Yes,
a gift of flowers is an expression of love or friendship, but why do
we usually enclose a card with a little message of greeting or sympathy? It is because even beautiful flowers cannot wholly take the
place of words—those words that are the real—*

BOUQUET OF LOVE

If loving thoughts and sentiments . . . Could make a bright
bouquet . . . Your vases would be filled, my love . . . With flowers
every day . . . The prettiest of flowers, dear . . . And in their fullest bloom . . . Enough for every corner of . . . Your porch and
every room . . . Enough for you to wear on gowns . . . And pin
up in your hair . . . And then some more to give your friends . . .
And scatter everywhere . . . Because my loving thoughts of you
. . . Are always more and more . . . They multiply until there is
. . . No way to keep the score . . . And they are just as beautiful
. . . And fragrant as the flowers . . . To tell my love and wish you
well . . . For all the years and hours.

When we marry we acquire another mother. If she is a real good mother (and she usually is), we do not think of her in the cold term of "mother-in-law." Personally, I always refer to her as my wife's mother, and to her I say—

I THANK YOU, MOTHER

Dear Mother, I am grateful for . . . The daughter that you raised . . . Both you and she deserve the best . . . And you should both be praised . . . I thank you for her gentleness . . . Her understanding way . . . And every sacrifice for me . . . She makes from day to day . . . Her loving smile, her helping hand . . . And every moment spent . . . With sympathy, devotion and . . . With true encouragement . . . Her guidance and protection to . . . The children as they grow . . . While telling them and showing them . . . The things they ought to know . . . I thank you, gracious Mother, for . . . The girl you brought to life . . . The princess fair, the charming one . . . Who is my lovely wife.

Some people have no compunction about taking unto themselves the credit that belongs to others. They do it by stealing ideas, claiming credit for someone else's success, or trying to "cut in on a good thing" by imitating it because they have no originality. May I never do that. I only want—

TO EARN MY LAURELS

Lord, let me not exalt my name . . . As human beings can . . . By seeking to assume the fame . . . Of some successful man . . . Let laurels come to me, O Lord . . . If any I deserve . . . According to the least reward . . . As I have tried to serve . . . For I would never steal his praise . . . Or basely imitate . . . The style or color of his ways . . . That made him truly great . . . I want to live my life and learn . . . How best I can achieve . . . And in all honesty to earn . . . The credit I receive . . . I would not scorch his living name . . . Or on his ashes stand . . . For all the generous acclaim . . . And glory of the land.

One of the greatest documents ever conceived and written is the Constitution of the United States. It is the framework of our government and our way of living. It is the sacred promise of our freedom on earth. Let us thank God and pay tribute to our forefathers on—

CONSTITUTION DAY

Today is Constitution Day . . . A time for celebration . . . Because the Constitution is . . . The backbone of our nation . . . Its articles, amendments and . . . Its special Bill of Rights . . . Are rungs along the ladder to . . . Our great and noble heights . . . And at the very top of it . . . In words that do not ramble . . . There is the stanchest rung of all . . . The glorious Preamble . . . The perfect Union, justice true . . . And home tranquillity . . . With welfare, freedom and defense . . . For our posterity . . . It is a solemn pledge that there . . . Will be no dissolution . . . God bless our land and help us to . . . Fulfill our Constitution.

It's wonderful to get a raise in pay, and surely it is an occasion for you and your wife to celebrate. But don't let it go to your head. Take it modestly, and hope for another one some day. Recognition of your ability, swift or slow, comes only—

AS YOU DESERVE

You get a raise in salary . . . And you go home today . . . And with your spouse you celebrate . . . The boosting of your pay . . . And as you figure to improve . . . The way in which you live . . . You dream that soon you will become . . . A big executive . . . And that is just the moment when . . . You have to keep your mind . . . And realize that each salary . . . Is set to meet each kind . . . You have to earn each raise in pay . . . And it may be a while . . . Before you have another chance . . . To celebrate and smile . . . So don't get too excited when . . . They elevate your pay . . . Your progress still depends upon . . . How well you win your way.

If you want to make an investment that will bring rich dividends without costing you a cent, be kind and gracious to those around you. A smile, a friendly word—it takes so little effort, and in that process of spreading happiness you discover a warm glow in your own heart. God will bless you for your—

✓ GRACIOUSNESS   *good*

Among the many qualities . . . And virtues we may stress . . . I think the happiest of all . . . Is that of graciousness . . . The gentle goodness of the heart . . . To smile and say hello . . . To every friend and relative . . . And those we may not know . . . To be considerate and kind . . . In every word and deed . . . And to anticipate and be . . . Prepared for every need . . . The gracious soul is one that proves . . . Its everlasting worth . . . By doing everything it can . . . For everyone on earth . . . And as we strive, we may be sure . . . That God will always bless . . . The home and the community . . . Where there is graciousness.

How long should a couple be engaged before they get married? The answer lies in the hearts of those who are promised to each other. It is up to them to decide, according to their self-assurance and their confidence in each other. They should be free of all doubt when they say—

LET'S GET MARRIED

Why must we wait a month or two . . . Or even one more day? . . . I love you with my heart and soul . . . What more is there to say? . . . I want to take you in my arms . . . And marry you right now . . . I want to hear your lips and mine . . . Repeat each sacred vow . . . You know that I belong to you . . . And you belong to me . . . So let us be together, love . . . Until eternity . . . There is no problem in your heart . . . I cannot solve with you . . . Our lives will be as one, my sweet . . . In everything we do . . . I cherish every smile you give . . . And every word you say . . . Oh, darling, please let nothing now . . . Delay our wedding day.

We do not like dust, and we try to get rid of it. Dust can spread disease, and in other ways it is unhealthy. But there will always be dust—even as we. "Remember, man, that thou art dust, and unto dust thou shalt return." Yes, we ourselves are the product of—

DUST

It settles on the furniture . . . The mantel and the floor . . . The pictures and the windows and . . . On every wall and door . . . It gathers at the ceiling where . . . The spider's web is spun . . . And everywhere it finds its share . . . Of glory in the sun . . . And that is why the world must have . . . Its mops and rags and brooms . . . And hands are busy at their task . . . Of renovating rooms . . . But whether it surrounds a hat . . . Or covers shiny shoes . . . It must at last be recognized . . . And given all its dues . . . For we are nothing more than that . . . However much we learn . . . And to its flimsy form some day . . . Our bodies must return.

What is more cheerful than a friendly letter—one that seems to converse with you and is genuinely interested in your welfare? Too many letters are filled with requests or demands, or they dwell boastingly on the sender. It is such a pleasant visit by mail when you receive that—

FRIENDLY LETTER

I got the nicest letter from . . . An old, old friend of mine . . . With just a bright and cheerful note . . . In every little line . . . He did not ask a favor and . . . He did not once complain . . . About misfortune in his life . . . Or any drop of rain . . . He merely said hello to me . . . And "How are you today?" . . . And "I do hope that everything . . . Is coming right your way" . . . I wish there were more letters that . . . The carrier would bring . . . As cheerful and as generous . . . Each time I hear his ring . . . And even more I wish that I . . . Could write a letter too . . . That did not concentrate on "me" . . . But only thought of "you."

Summer is over, and now we begin the third part of God's calendar —beautiful autumn. The leaves are changing to a blaze of magic colors. Soon the wind will seem a little stronger, and the leaves will grow weaker as they start to fall on the ground. There is a wistfulness that draws this season close to the heart. Sincerely and sentimentally we—

THANK GOD FOR AUTUMN

The leaves are changing colors now . . . The autumn days are here . . . And life assumes a thoughtful and . . . More lively atmosphere . . . It is the season God ordained . . . For newborn energies . . . Commingled with the peacefulness . . . Of wistful memories . . . There is a touch of loneliness . . . As summer days depart . . . But there are many joys and songs . . . To fill the human heart . . . The harvest field, the vineyard ripe . . . The pumpkins everywhere . . . Thanksgiving Day and Halloween . . . And snowflakes in the air . . . Thank God for autumn with its shades . . . Of russet, green and gold . . . And all of nature's glories we . . . Are privileged to behold.

Praise and gratitude are among the most powerful means we have to encourage each other to greater and nobler deeds. These flowers for the living are an inspiration not only to the recipient but likewise to all who are thereby reminded of his charity or other accomplishment. Let us be timely in saying—

GOD LOVE YOU

God love you for your kindness and . . . Your helpfulness today . . . God love you for your charity . . . In every thoughtful way . . . Your contribution does so much . . . To guide another soul . . . To happiness and holiness . . . And its eternal goal . . . Your action is a sacrifice . . . As much as it can be . . . And God will give you credit in . . . His great eternity . . . God love you for remembering . . . Your fellow men on earth . . . And giving recognition to . . . Their own and equal worth . . . You are at once an angel and . . . A king upon this sod . . . You are a saint in Heaven and . . . A messenger from God.

*Can life ever be as wonderful as a fairy tale? Yes, if we are deeply
in love with each other, and if our love endures above everything
else. Our castle of dreams will become a reality, and there will always
be a rainbow around our hearts, as we live—*

OUR STORY BOOK

Our life is like a story book . . . Where fairy tales come true . . .
And every pretty picture is . . . A photograph of you . . . The
titles of our chapters are . . . The silver stars above . . . And every
paragraph is one . . . Of happiness and love . . . The letters are
like diamonds . . . The periods are pearls . . . The commas and
the question marks . . . Are lovely golden curls . . . Our castle
reaches to the sky . . . With flowers all around . . . Its stairs are
made of memories . . . That started from the ground . . . The
covers of our story book . . . Are doors to love and laughter . . .
Where you are in my arms and we . . . Are happy ever after.

*"Skid Row" is the urban sea of human derelicts, but not all such
ghost ships are to be sighted there. Some drift around on the streams
of active, everyday life. They are those individuals who work without accomplishing anything, who are selfish and indifferent, and
have no interest in anyone or anything around them. They are—*

THE USELESS SOULS

There is no greater tragedy . . . And rarely an excuse . . . For
anyone upon this earth . . . Of no or little use . . . The one who
really wastes his life . . . Ignores his neighborhood . . . And does
not try in any way . . . To do a little good . . . There are the
mental cases and . . . The fault is not their own . . . But there are
those indifferent ones . . . Whose minds are fully grown . . . The
ones who do not want to work . . . Or ever get ahead . . . And
never care or worry if . . . They are alive or dead . . . They are
the parasites who beg . . . Or hang around for doles . . . They
are the lazy, selfish ones . . . They are the useless souls.

The chain grocery and big department store are indeed an eco-
nomical boon, but I have a warm spot in my heart for that little
neighborhood store. While this or that may cost a few pennies more,
there is a friendliness and closeness that cannot be matched by the
giant sales place. That's why I like the—

CORNER STORE

When there is something that we need . . . And we are looking
for . . . We always like to patronize . . . The little corner store
. . . The humble store that stands upon . . . The corner near our
home . . . Without the slightest modern touch . . . Of fancy tile
or chrome . . . It may not carry merchandise . . . In such variety
. . . As those that are so far removed . . . From our community
. . . It may not have the atmosphere . . . Of Paris or New York
. . . Or have the social etiquette . . . That lifts the salad fork . . .
And as against some big ones, it . . . May charge a little more . . .
But we prefer to patronize . . . The little corner store.

Everything has its compensations, like eating at home or dining
out. It usually costs less to eat at home, and you have the coziness
of the family gathering. On the other hand, there is that change of
pace and the absence of dirty dishes when you have—

DINNER OUT

We like to eat our dinner out . . . Whenever we are tired . . .
And when there is no special cook . . . Or servant to be hired . . .
Or when we have a reason for . . . A real good celebration . . .
And toss aside the budget book . . . Without examination . . .
But those are rare occasions and . . . We seldom splurge or squan-
der . . . Because we do not like to see . . . Our dimes and dollars
wander . . . We much prefer to stay at home . . . With meat and
mashed potatoes . . . A bowl of soup, a piece of pie . . . And dressing on tomatoes . . . But when we do go out to eat . . . Some
steaks or fancy fishes . . . We love it and we worry not . . . About
the dirty dishes.

kindly

Why do some people think unpleasant thoughts? How can it make them happy? Isn't it much easier to dwell upon the joys of life, to hope instead of despair, and to feel kindly toward others? We live as we think. So let us strive to be cheerful and unselfish in all—

OUR THOUGHTS

Our thoughts are free and they can be . . . As secret as the night . . . For they are ever silent and . . . Forever out of sight . . . Unless we put them into words . . . On paper or in speech . . . And thereby move our mind within . . . Another person's reach . . . But it is up to us to choose . . . Whatever we would think . . . To narrow down our chain of thought . . . Or add another link . . . Then why not take the pleasant thoughts . . . The gracious and the kind . . . And leave the vain, the selfish and . . . The hateful ones behind? . . . For as we think, so do we live . . . And gain or lose our goal . . . And so God's final judgment will . . . Be passed upon our soul.

However dark and uncertain the outlook for ourselves, our nation or the world, we still and always have the consolation of our faith in God. Even our coin of the realm reminds us, "In God we trust." The world will come to an end some day but maybe not now, if we believe and trust, and if we say a—

PRAYER IN OUR TIME

In these uncertain days, O Lord . . . These nights so filled with fear . . . Give us the wisdom to appraise . . . The words we read and hear . . . Let not our hearts become confused . . . Let not our souls be lulled . . . By false impressions, hopes and dreams . . . Until our wits are dulled . . . Give us the courage to go on . . . The way we have been taught . . . With freedom, faith and charity . . . In every daily thought . . . With life as we have known its joy . . . And every common ache . . . In opportunities for us . . . And for our children's sake . . . Let not the mind of mortal man . . . Be buried under rust . . . Let not the spire of our prayer . . . Be crumbled into dust.

[*145*]

America's newspaper boy is one of our greatest traditions. Scores of successful men started out in life by peddling papers on the street or tossing them onto porches. An honorable occupation, it is a youngster's first introduction to business. We love that boy because—

HE SURE DELIVERS

God bless the busy boy who brings . . . The paper to our door . . . Who earns his daily profit and . . . Who asks for nothing more . . . He is in business for himself . . . As much as anyone . . . And he is really learning how . . . That business should be run . . . He has to give the service that . . . His customers demand . . . And keep a proper record of . . . The cash and checks on hand . . . He has to sacrifice at least . . . A portion of his play . . . While keeping up his schoolwork and . . . His paper route each day . . . And so our hearts are grateful for . . . Our comfort, pride and joy . . . With every headline we receive . . . From our newspaper boy.

Every month holds a special meaning for someone, and some of us find a special meaning in every month. One of my special months is October, because it is the month in which she was born—she who is my love and the mother of our children. And so I always say to her—

THANKS IN OCTOBER

Once more it is October, dear . . . And I remember you . . . The only one who had the gift . . . To make my dreams come true . . . The dreams of peace and comfort and . . . A little of success . . . A soft caress, a loving kiss . . . And time for happiness . . . The dream of flowers in a vase . . . A fragrant kitchen smell . . . And then the chiming of the clock . . . To tell that all is well . . . The dream of childish laughter at . . . The turning of the stair . . . And all of us together in . . . The whisper of a prayer . . . Once more it is October, dear . . . And I repeat to you . . . My ever- because . . . You made my dreams come true.

Yes, the year is like a day. As mentioned on the January, April and July pages of this book, the year has its dawn, its late morning, and its afternoon. Now that day is drawing to a close. This is our final opportunity to make up for lost time, to prove forever that this year was not in vain, as we begin—

YEAR'S EVENING

The shades of afternoon are drawn . . . And gradually they blend . . . With twilight and our final chance . . . Before this day must end . . . This is the evening of the year . . . In which to carry on . . . Before the daylight disappears . . . And twelve more months are gone . . . Yes, every day is like a year . . . It seems to go that fast . . . And when the sun goes down, the year . . . Is buried in the past . . . There still is time to make amends . . . And to achieve our goal . . . If we have confidence in God . . . And courage in our soul . . . So let us keep our struggle up . . . Or strive to start anew . . . Almighty God will credit us . . . For everything we do.

October 4

It is only human to look back over the years and wonder how life would have turned out if we had done things differently. Usually we think we overpassed a better opportunity, especially if we are dissatisfied with our present lot. But we could be wrong, and we might have been a lot worse off. So—

WHY WONDER?

So many of us wonder what . . . Our life today would be . . . If somewhere in the past our minds . . . Had chosen differently . . . We might have been superior . . . In body and in health . . . We might have gathered glory and . . . A good amount of wealth . . . We might have married someone else . . . And had a better mate . . . And in a dozen other ways . . . Improved our earthly state . . . But do we ever stop to think . . . About the other side? . . . It could have been a whole lot worse . . . And even that we died . . . So why regret the years gone by . . . Or fear the years to live? . . . When God is there with all the grace . . . He is prepared to give.

What is an allergy? As between the present and past generations, it is still a mystery. We had no allergies in the old days. We all got along all right. Or did we? Maybe we had allergies without knowing it, and maybe some unsolved tragedies in those days could have been prevented, had doctors discovered—

ALLERGIES

We used to keep our bodies well . . . With common remedies
. . . But now it seems we have to fight . . . A world of allergies
. . . Our little boy is not so well . . . His sister is the same . . .
And there is nothing else on earth . . . But allergy to blame . . .
He can not swallow milk to get . . . The calcium he needs . . .
She has to stay away from oil . . . Derived from cotton seeds . . .
They dare not sleep on feathers or . . . Enjoy a chocolate snack
. . . For those are bound to bring about . . . A violent attack . . .
Our doctors seem so expert now . . . To keep the body strong . . .
We can not help but wonder how . . . We used to get along.

We are on this earth only by the grace of God. Any moment He may call us. The important thing in life is that we do His holy will, and while we are here we should thank Him for His blessings and ask forgiveness for our failures. Knowing that death is certain, we ought to pray—

BUT IF I LIVE

This day, O Lord, consider me . . . For what I may be worth
. . . According to my pleasures and . . . My penance on this earth
. . . According to the balance of . . . My scales on Judgment Day
. . . If now my soul is summoned and . . . My body pass away
. . . But if You let me live, O Lord . . . A little longer now . . .
Forgive me for my failures and . . . My every broken vow . . .
Consider now the frailty . . . That soothes and softens me . . . As
much as weakness is a part . . . Of all humanity . . . And give me
strength to carry on . . . And do Your holy will   That I may
keep your word, and all   My promises fulfill.

Would you mind turning back to August 18 in this ᴀ
talking about, "My Little Girl," and how girls are sweet. ᴠ
say they are, but I must admit that now and then they geₜ
hair, and they can get away with anything. And yet I love

LITTLE GIRL

A little girl is something sweet . . . That comes upon this earth
. . . To interrupt and balance life . . . With misery and mirth
. . . She always gets into your hair . . . When you are occupied
. . . And when you want to be alone . . . She never leaves your
side . . . You have to hug her dollies and . . . Adore her party
dress . . . And every ice cream cone you buy . . . Becomes a lovely
mess . . . She sings and dances all day long . . . Until she falls
asleep . . . But when you want her to perform . . . She won't let
out a peep . . . And whether she is giggling or . . . Deliberately
she cries . . . You cannot scold her when you see . . . Those soft,
enchanting eyes.

October 8

The years have flown, but the memories remain in your heart. You
dream back, and you wish it could have turned out that way, but it
didn't, and perhaps it was your fault. Now it is too late—too late to
whisper again: I love you—

MY WONDERFUL ONE

I wish with all my heart and soul . . . That it were not this way
. . . I wish that it were long ago . . . A magic yesterday . . . A
yesterday of years gone by . . . When lilacs bloomed in spring . . .
And there was only one sweet song . . . We ever cared to sing . . .
Do you remember it, my love? . . . Do you remember me? . . .
My wonderful and only one . . . As dear as you could be? . . . I
hear the record playing now . . . I see your soft brown eyes . . . I
take you in my arms again . . . And listen to your sighs . . . I kiss
your sweet and loving lips . . . I hold you to my heart . . . And
then the song is ended and . . . Again we are apart.

The Great Chicago Fire took place in 1871. It lasted from October 8 to 11. That tragic event now determines Fire Prevention Week as the week in which October 9 falls, a date decided upon arbitrarily. This day, and every day, let us do all we can to—

PREVENT THE FLAME

Why take a chance with fire when . . . The risk is always great . . . And just one second may become . . . One second just too late? . . . It takes so little of our time . . . To safeguard trash and waste . . . And check on all electric things . . . Without a bit of haste . . . One little careless match could set . . . A continent on fire . . . And if the oceans were not there . . . The world might by a pyre . . . In home and office, factory . . . The forest and the street . . . Let our defense against each spark . . . Be speedy and complete . . . And if we hope to save our lives . . . And really want to win . . . Let us prevent the smallest flame . . . Before it can begin.

There is nothing worse than betraying a friend, or to cast aside friendship for no reason at all. True friendship is based on brotherly love—the mutual willingness to serve and sacrifice, whenever, wherever. I pray to be—

FOREVER FAITHFUL

Whatever I may do in life . . . Unto its farthest end . . . I pray that I shall never be . . . Unfaithful to a friend . . . If anyone is kind to me . . . By any night or day . . . I feel it is a favor I . . . Should happily repay . . . And whether he has helped me out . . . In anything at all . . . I am a faithful friend to him . . . At every beck and call . . . As long as he is kind to me . . . And helps my heart to live . . . There is not anything in life . . . I would not gladly give . . . As much as I am healthy and . . . My life I may expend . . . I pray that I shall never be . . . Unfaithful to a friend.

It happens so often that it seems to be always. The phone rings, and where are you? Usually you are quite removed, and you cannot reach the instrument in time. Or else it rings right in your ear, and the call is a nuisance call that disturbs your rest. You cannot outguess the phone. Somehow always—

THE RINGS ARE WRONG

Each time the phone starts ringing I . . . Am far away from it . . . And as I dash to pick it up . . . It suddenly has quit . . . It happens when I take a bath . . . Or when I step outside . . . Or any time I am removed . . . Beyond a normal stride . . . And then there are occasions when . . . I like a little peace . . . And sure enough it starts to ring . . . And never does it cease . . . I wish there were a gadget that . . . Could gauge the mood and mind . . . And guide the telephone to be . . . Considerate and kind . . . I hear an endless loud alarm . . . Or just a ding-a-ling . . . And neither seems to match my mind . . . Or mood for answering.

We owe the beginning of our freedom to the colonists—the sons and daughters of the Pilgrims who settled upon this continent. But how would the Pilgrims have known about this continent unless Columbus had discovered it? Let us commemorate and say—

GOD BLESS COLUMBUS

Thank God for this Columbus Day . . . Thank God in every way . . . That we have our America . . . Where we may work and pray . . . Thank God for our United States . . . Our freedom of the press . . . And for the liberty in our . . . Pursuit of happiness . . . Columbus had the courage great . . . To sail the widest sea . . . And by his daring exploits we . . . Record our history . . . We had to conquer tyranny . . . To make this land our own . . . And we deserve the credit for . . . The way that it has grown . . . But Christopher Columbus was . . . The one who led the way . . . And for his faith and fortitude . . . We honor him today.

What more can you offer your beloved than to promise everything you can possibly do for him or her? Maybe your word is doubted, and maybe someday you will break that promise, but the most that can be asked of anyone is the loving sentiment: I will do—

WHATEVER YOU WISH

Whatever I can do for you . . . Is part of every vow . . . Whatever I have promised, dear . . . I want to do it now . . . I offer you my happy heart . . . And that is all of me . . . Except my body and the mind . . . That holds my memory . . . And these are also yours to have . . . As much as I can give . . . I am your own, my dearest one . . . As long as I may live . . . With loving lips I kiss your feet . . . I am your servant true . . . And there is nothing on this earth . . . I would not do for you . . . As much as I am capable . . . On any sea or land . . . Wherever I may be with you . . . Your wish is my command.

Kristina means well, but what can you expect of a little girl when it comes to social obligations? I keep after her, trying to get her to write those thank-you notes for gifts and cards received, but she is like any girl her age—too busy to bother with writing. And so, inevitably, it is my job to write and say—

SHE THANKS YOU

Kristina sends her thank-you notes . . . And writes them very well . . . Though now and then her gratitude . . . Is left for me to tell . . . She is so happy to receive . . . The gifts from far and near . . . And her appreciation is . . . So deep and so sincere . . . But like the average little girl . . . She has so much to do . . . That sometimes she neglects to say . . . Her loving thanks to you . . . And then I have to take her place . . . To let the sender know . . . The package was delivered and . . . Her eyes were all aglow . . . So if you get a note of thanks . . . I send you in her name . . . It really is her sentiment . . . And I am not to blame.

Times change as we go through life. Custom and habit change, and sometimes even our whole way of living becomes different. But that is life, and we must put away the things of our younger days if we want to get ahead. There is no turning back, as life goes—

ALWAYS ONWARD

The streets are not the same today . . . As those I used to know . . . And different are the cities now . . . Where I would like to go . . . My views have changed since I was young . . . The world has turned around . . . And I am not beholden to . . . The way where I was bound . . . But that is only natural . . . For as we live and learn . . . There are so many other things . . . For which we deeply yearn . . . We want to probe the problems and . . . To solve the mysteries . . . From home to school and heaven and . . . Beyond the seven seas . . . And so as I go on each day . . . And leave another track . . . I walk into the future and . . . There is no turning back.

Sometimes when someone dies, the bereaved request relatives and friends to omit flowers at the funeral and to contribute the cost of such blooms to charity. But how many persons mail their checks? And, after all, why shouldn't there be flowers, with their tribute to God as well as to the dead? Think it over and—

PLEASE DON'T OMIT

Sometimes when people pass away . . . And we are told of it . . . We are implored upon to pray . . . But—"flowers please omit" . . . And though their words may truly mean . . . To help some charity . . . They do forget each seed is part . . . Of God's sublimity . . . God made the flowers everywhere . . . Of every shape and hue . . . And when we place them on a grave . . . We do Him honor too . . . Each rose or gladiolus or . . . The humblest daffodil . . . Is one more fragrant handiwork . . . According to His will . . . And as they blossom in the home . . . Or _____ the sod . . . So do they speak of life and death . . . W_____ tude to God.

No matter how humble your job, how simple your work, there is always the possibility that your personality or your efforts will be recognized. You may think you are forgotten or ignored. But you never know. There is—

ALWAYS A CHANCE

Sometimes a clerk is just a jerk . . . A steno is a dame . . . And as they toil from day to day . . . Their titles are the same . . . But now and then a youngster will . . . Amaze his doubting boss . . . By building up his profit and . . . By cutting down his loss . . . By coming up with some idea . . . Comparatively new . . . To help the company achieve . . . The thing it wants to do . . . And now and then some steno will . . . Advance a theory . . . To bring in bigger business or . . . Promote economy . . . And so there always is a chance . . . No matter who we are . . . To reach into the universe . . . And touch a silver star.

Wouldn't it be wonderful if you and your loved one could be together all of every day and night? Yes, but you have to go to work, and except for week ends, holidays and vacations, you have to wait for the sun to go down before you can be with her. Lovingly you remind her: This has to be the story of—

OUR DAY AND NIGHT

The day is mine, the night is yours . . . As we may be together . . . Not by the chance of cruel fate . . . Or any change of weather . . . It is a simple fact that I . . . Must labor every day . . . To try to get ahead in life . . . And multiply my pay . . . And so I have to go to work . . . And struggle through the hours . . . When I would rather kiss your lips . . . And shower you with flowers . . . But in my heart and in my dreams . . . You never are away . . . You are forever at my side . . . Throughout the working day . . . The day is mine, the night is yours . . . Yet both are ours to treasure . . . Because my daily dreams of you . . . Become our nightly pleasure.

It happens to all of us now and then. We are seated in a restaurant. The waiter brings bread and water, takes our order, and then he vanishes. He is never around when we want him, but when it's time to pay the check and leave a tip, he suddenly appears out of nowhere. More than once during dinner we want to scream—

WAITER!

The waiter is a creature who . . . Is always disappearing . . . And who, when he is visible . . . Is never within hearing . . . He brings you bread and water on . . . A special silver tray . . . And promises your order will . . . Be filled without delay . . . The soup is served, the salad too . . . And you are quite elated . . . But after that the minutes are . . . The hours you have waited . . . And so it goes throughout the meal . . . Until you grab your hat . . . And then the waiter, check in hand . . . Is there in nothing flat . . . Of course there is the creature who . . . Deserves a tip for service . . . But long before he gets it, you . . . Are dubious and nervous.

Once in a while when you go to church, or when you whisper to God in your home or as you walk along the street, pray not just for yourself, your loved ones and your friends, but think of others, and ask God's help—

FOR ALL THE WORLD

I say this prayer to You, My God . . . For all the world today . . . That all the world may strive to live . . . According to Your way . . . That atheists, agnostics and . . . All humans who are blind . . . May see The Light, and It may touch . . . And penetrate each mind . . . That Christians may improve their ways . . . And Jews be true to You . . . As those with fervent faith and hope . . . Have always tried to do . . . I say this prayer that all may live . . . In peace and liberty . . . And You will give Your blessing now . . . To all humanity . . . Be with us, God, however far . . . Our thoughts and dreams may reach . . . And help us all to follow the . . . Commandments that You teach.

How thoughtless, how ungrateful we are! We have our comforts,
our conveniences and our joys from day to day, but they make little,
if any, impression on us until they are suddenly taken away. We do
not appreciate our blessings—

UNTIL TOO LATE

We never quite appreciate . . . Our happiness each day . . .
Until some tragedy occurs . . . To take our joy away . . . We take
our life for granted and . . . Believe that it will be . . . An ordinary path on earth . . . To peace and harmony . . . But suddenly
our path is changed . . . And we are not prepared . . . To fight
for every human right . . . For which we ever cared . . . And then
at last we realize what . . . We had and what we lost . . . And
what we have to sacrifice . . . To pay the final cost . . . So let us
all be conscious of . . . Our blessings every day . . . And do our
best with prayer and zest . . . To keep it just that way.

The wonderful thing about having friends is that they are always
with you, at least in spirit. You may not see or speak to them every
day, but you know that their names are in the phone book and in
your diary. In my own case they are even closer—they are always—

IN MY HEART

My friends are in the phone book and . . . They fill my friendship file . . . And in a dozen diaries . . . I see their every smile
. . . Their faces are the pictures in . . . The scrapbook that I keep
. . . The memories that come to life . . . Each time I go to sleep
. . . They are the happy thoughts I have . . . From morning until
night . . . And all the influence I need . . . To keep my thinking
right . . . They comfort me when I am down . . . They help me
to get up . . . And in their good companionship . . . I drink no
bitter cup . . . My friends may be at home with me . . . Or we
may be apart . . . But whether here or there, my friends . . . Are
always in my heart.

Today is my wife's birthday. It is her special day of the year, and yet this day is just as much my own, because she belongs to me. I am grateful to God for having created her, and I thank her that she accepted me, as I whisper to her: Happy Birthday, my love, on this—

YOUR DAY AND MINE

It is your birthday, dearest one . . . And yet it is my day . . . Because your happiness is mine . . . In such a special way . . . When you are happy in your heart . . . Then I am truly glad . . . Just as the tears that touch your cheek . . . Are those that make me sad . . . When there is sunshine in your eyes . . . It smiles into my heart . . . And I am lonely only when . . . We have to be apart . . . And so my birthday wish for you . . . Is one that favors me . . . And magnifies my every joy . . . In your dear company . . . But I express it first for you . . . And fervently I say . . . God love you, dear, as I love you . . . Today and every day.

Some bosses are flattered to be called by their initials, and their underlings know that. And some bosses are not complimented at all, because they know the underlings are "polishing the apple." It is sort of in-between, and when you come right down to it—

WHAT'S IN INITIALS?

One day we got to thinking and . . . We said, "What's in a name?" . . . And after that the meaning of . . . A name was not the same . . . But there are still initials that . . . Are plaguing you and me . . . Regarding business bosses and . . . The ones in industry . . . "Hello, J. B.," "Good night, C. C."—"A call for you, R. O." . . . Which indicates the boss is one . . . You intimately know . . . He may be pleased but usually . . . It is the apple bright . . . That someone plucked the day before . . . And polished up all night . . . And usually he knows it and . . . It is a total loss . . . For one who tries to lean on those . . . Initials of his boss.

The joy of love is to live for the one you love. Your heart wants to give itself unselfishly to that other heart—now and forever—as you declare: I want to live for you and—

TO LIVE WITH YOU

Your love is my enchanting vase . . . Your smiles are all my flowers . . . And all around the clock you are . . . My minutes and my hours . . . You are the magic of my day . . . From dawn to candlelight . . . And you are all the tiny stars . . . That twinkle through the night . . . I dream of you, I cherish you . . . Whatever tide or weather . . . And all I hope and pray is just . . . That we may be together . . . I want you for myself as much . . . As I may comfort you . . . And you are welcome to my heart . . . In everything I do . . . I want to live my life with you . . . Forever and forever . . . To hold you in my loving arms . . . And never leave you—never.

Do you remember the story of the ten lepers who were made clean, and only one returned to Jesus to give thanks? "But where are the nine?" asked Jesus. How true that is of our daily life! In time of distress we turn to God for help, but how often do we thank Him for blessings received? Now and then—

WHY NOT THANK GOD?

When we are troubled in our hearts . . . We turn to God and pray . . . With faith and hope and tearful wish . . . In every word we say . . . We turn to God for comfort when . . . The storm is at our door . . . And when the waves of fear and stress . . . Would wash away our shore . . . But when the world is beautiful . . . And life is sweet and whole . . . And when there is no obstacle . . . To keep us from our goal . . . How often do we realize that . . . Success is not our own? . . . That every glory on this earth . . . Belongs to God alone? . . . How often do we thank Him for . . . Our daily happiness . . . Instead of always ng Him . . . To help us in distress?

Life from day to day may seem monotonous. But when that life is at home, in the heart of a happy family, the monotony of daily routine is wonderful. Yes, there are problems, including bills to be paid, but where could we buy the peaceful security of love in the family circle? That is how my wife, the children and I feel about—

OUR LIFE AT HOME

Our life at home is just the same . . . Whatever month or day . . . The problems of our children and . . . The bills we have to pay . . . The season makes no difference and . . . Vacation does not matter . . . While every dream of easy life . . . Is only so much chatter . . . The struggle never lessens and . . . The task is never light . . . It starts with every morning and . . . It never says good night . . . And yet there is a comfort in . . . The changing of the weather . . . Because whatever kind it is . . . We always are together . . . And as we have our health and home . . . And God is there to bless . . . So we are grateful in our hearts . . . For love and happiness.

Not all echoes emanate from mountains, valleys or the walls of some buildings. Indeed, there are echoes inaudible to the ear, but they can be heard by the heart. They are the sounds of yesterday, of hopes and dreams, of smiles and tears. Many a memory becomes an—

ECHO

An echo is the mirror that . . . Reflects the smallest sounds . . . It is the voice that strikes a rock . . . And instantly rebounds . . . It issues from the mountainside . . . Or from a hollow hall . . . The valley of a deep ravine . . . Or some acoustic wall . . . But also there are echoes that . . . No science can explain . . . The echoes of a yesterday . . . In sunshine or in rain . . . The echo of a happy song . . . That glorified the day . . . The echo of a lonely soul . . . That never goes away . . . There are a thousand echoes, and . . . Each echo plays its part . . . But none is greater than the one . . . That speaks the human heart.

There is no true love without humility—the humility of your grati-
de for the love bestowed upon you. It should not be the kind that
says, "I am not worthy of you," but just the honest acknowledgment
that you are not better than someone else. Let that feeling be mutual
as you embrace your love and say: Darling—

HOLD ME CLOSE

You offered all you had to give . . . You gave yourself to me . . .
And then you hoped and prayed that I . . . Would listen to your
plea . . . My darling, it is not your lips . . . But mine that should
be speaking . . . To ask for all the happiness . . . That every heart
is seeking . . . I should be humble at your feet . . . And looking
up to you . . . And that is everything I wish . . . That you would
let me do . . . Because you are so wonderful . . . By every golden
measure . . . And just to take you in my arms . . . Would be a
lasting treasure . . . I want you more than all the world . . . Or
any little part . . . My darling, I am yours to hold . . . Please hold
me to your heart.

You may never know who your neighbors are, and you may never
find out unless you say hello to them. They could become your best
friends of the future. Why not find out? Why not—

BE NEIGHBORLY

Your neighbor is familiar or . . . A person strange and new . . .
Across the street, just down the block . . . Or right next door to you
. . . Your neighbor is a creature who . . . Is not unlike yourself
. . . With house to clean, and groceries . . . To stack upon the
shelf . . . With wage to earn, the children's care . . . The doctor,
school and church . . . And with that goal of joy and peace . . .
For which all humans search . . . Your neighbor can assist you in
. . . Your trouble and distress . . . And add a little brighter touch
. . . To all your happiness . . . So why not be more neighborly
. . . And pleasant through and through? . . . Your neighbor may
be longing to . . . Be neighborly with you.

Centuries ago the eve of All Saints' Day was a time of witchcraft, when atheists sought to invoke curses on all who believed in God. Now it is an occasion of harmless celebration, especially for children. It is a night of fun—

IT'S HALLOWEEN

Tonight belongs to children of . . . The ages small and teen . . . It is the time they celebrate . . . Their happy Halloween . . . The witches ride upon their brooms . . . The jack-o'-lanterns leer . . . The goblins gape but youngsters know . . . There is no cause for fear . . . They wear their masks and costumes gay . . . As they go down the street . . . And lean on bells or knock on doors . . . To holler "trick or treat" . . . It is a harmless bit of fun . . . As it is done today . . . Especially if you and I . . . Co-operate and pay . . . So let us have some candy, fruit . . . Or cookies in our hands . . . To please the merry boys and girls . . . And meet their small demands.

Few things are more frightening than losing a job. Sometimes it seems as though your world is coming to an end. And yet, so often when you lose a job, you find a better one. Getting fired, or being released for other reasons, may turn out to be a blessing in disguise. So don't worry too much about—

LOSING A JOB

It is not always a disgrace . . . To lose a certain job . . . And certainly no cause in life . . . To sit around and sob . . . I had a dozen jobs or more . . . Of which I quickly tired . . . And if I did not quit the task . . . I usually got fired . . . From day to day and coast to coast . . . There is the noble name . . . Of one who was discharged before . . . He rose to wealth and fame . . . I do not mean that losing jobs . . . Is something to be treasured . . . But it is not the final rule . . . By which a man is measured . . . And I may never reach the height . . . Of glory in the sun . . . But every time I lost a job . . . I got a better one.

How often do you remember and pray for your loved ones who have passed from this earth? They need your prayers now, more than they ever did in life, and when your time comes, you will be needing theirs. Remember to—

PRAY FOR THE DEAD

How often do we think about . . . Our dear ones who are dead . . . And take the time to ask our God . . . To keep them comforted? . . . How often do we pray for those . . . Whose lives are now no more . . . That they may intercede for us . . . To pass through Heaven's door? . . . They know the reason for this life . . . The mystery of death . . . And God's reward or punishment . . . For every human breath . . . No matter what we think about . . . Our future or today . . . Let us be mindful of the time . . . When we must pass away . . . And let us pray for those who are . . . In God's eternity . . . That they may have a kindly word . . . To say for you and me.

We have a main phone and two extensions, and that is quite a convenience around the house. But what we really need are three or four main lines to overcome that juvenile interference. Our really important calls are impossible when there are—

KIDS ON THE PHONE

The phone is meant to be a means . . . Of quick communication . . . To expedite important news . . . And urgent information . . . And everywhere it also serves . . . To say a fond hello . . . To relatives and loving friends . . . And anyone we know . . . In either case our use of it . . . Should be succinct and sparing . . . Especially when on a line . . . That other folks are sharing . . . But when the youngsters pick it up . . . They never put it down . . . They either talk an hour or . . . They call all over town . . . And whether it is local or . . . To some suburban station . . . The message of a boy or girl . . . Is merely conversation.

Patience is one of the greatest virtues in life. It is the ability to bear up under trials and ordeals, and to put up with the faults in others that annoy you. No one knows that better than I, as my wife puts up with me, and I say to her constantly: Thank you—

FOR YOUR PATIENCE

I love you for the sweetness of . . . Our moments all alone . . . Your faith and hope but most of all . . . The patience you have shown . . . You have believed in me, and you . . . Have hoped that someday I . . . Would make a name for both of us . . . To write across the sky . . . You have been patient through the years . . . You never once complained . . . Because I seemed too occupied . . . Or just because it rained . . . You never asked or doubted me . . . Or tried to search my soul . . . As I continued on my way . . . To reach a greater goal . . . I love you for your patience, dear . . . I give my thanks to you . . . And you deserve the credit for . . . Whatever I may do.

Some day, if you live long enough, you are going to be old. When you reach that stage, you will be glad that some people still remember and take an interest in you. Meanwhile, why not give a thought now and then to those who already belong to the—

GOLDEN AGE GROUP

God bless the ones who have attained . . . The happy, golden age . . . Where they relive the memories . . . Of every faded page . . . The silver-haired and weary group . . . Of women and of men . . . Who wish for all that they might do . . . If they could live again . . . They are the ones who probably . . . Have done the best they could . . . And who are only interested . . . In doing still more good . . . Who want to help this world along . . . To find a better way . . . To freedom, truth and justice and . . . Equality today . . . They are the kindly folks who are . . . About to leave the stage . . . May God be generous to them . . . In this their golden age.

There are only two ways of life—the selfish and the unselfish. Either we love God and our neighbor, or we love ourselves. The only real happy medium is that of gathering joy to our hearts by doing good for others. That is the only path to—

OUR PLEASURE

The pleasures of this life on earth . . . Are really only two . . . According to the way we think . . . And what we strive to do . . . We hurry to the happiness . . . Of laughter and of fun . . . Frivolity and revelry . . . Where nothing else is done . . . Or else we seek the peaceful joy . . . Of doing what is right . . . With friendship to our neighbor and . . . With mercy in the night . . . We live our lives for other souls . . . In sunshine or in rain . . . Or we pursue the path to greed . . . And every selfish gain . . . There is no pleasure to be had . . . Beyond this choice of two . . . To please ourselves or honor God . . . In everything we do.

Sympathy is the kiss of neighborly love. It is the heart that opens and the hand that reaches out in time of sorrow. It is at once the richest and least costly gift we can bestow. Let us always be generous with—

OUR SYMPATHY

The quality of sympathy . . . Is virtuous and good . . . In every home and family . . . And every neighborhood . . . In time of stress or sorrow or . . . Of sudden tragedy . . . It is an act of mercy and . . . A deed of charity . . . To give ourselves to others in . . . The hour of their tears . . . And try to calm their troubled hearts . . . And take away their fears . . . It is the least that we can give . . . To those who are in pain . . . To suffer with them in our soul . . . Our body and our brain . . . To share their misery and fate . . . Unto the last degree . . . If only by the feeling of . . . Our human sympathy.

The right to vote may not impress you much, but you, whether you realize it or not, has an important bearing on yo. and the lives of your family and your neighbors. Read up a lit politics, study the candidates, and when you go to cast your bunot, say a—

VOTER'S PRAYER

I pray that I shall cast my vote . . . The way it ought to be . . . At least that it will help preserve . . . Our life and liberty . . . Whichever candidate may win . . . Or party may succeed . . . I want the ballot that I cast . . . To be my honest deed . . . I may be right, I may be wrong . . . As I have thought or guessed . . . But I just hope my choice will be . . . The one who is the best . . . I want to do my duty as . . . A voter in this land . . . However much all politics . . . Are hard to understand . . . I pray to God my vote will not . . . Be cast upon the sea . . . But it will help preserve our life . . . Of truth and liberty.

November 9

He may not admit it, but many a boss envies the office boy with his carefree life and lack of responsibility. When he was an office boy, he envied his boss, and he was filled with ambition. But the higher he rose, the more burdens he had to shoulder, and finally— maybe—he wonders why he ever wanted—

TO GET AHEAD

I used to hate that office work . . . When I was just a boy . . . But if it were my task today . . . It would be quite a joy . . . I used to dream of being boss . . . And running all the firm . . . Of supervising everything . . . And watching others squirm . . . And then I forged ahead, although . . . I did it luckily . . . And found that I was burdened with . . . Responsibility . . . I had to make decisions bold . . . Without the slightest aid . . . And all my future hinged upon . . . The progress that I made . . . I often wish that I were back . . . To office work each day . . . To simply follow orders and . . . To get my humble pay.

The holy vow of matrimony binds two hearts together—forever and forever. Once that sacred vow is spoken, there should be no place for doubt or mistrust. There should be perfect faith and confidence. as we have said—

OUR HOLY VOW

Your love is mine because I know . . . That God is in your heart . . . As much as you have promised me . . . That we will never part . . . As much as you have said to me . . . That we will be together . . . Whatever hour of the day . . . Or changing of the weather . . . Your love is mine, and mine is yours . . . As much as I can give . . . I am your own forever, dear . . . As long as I may live . . . I do not ever doubt your word . . . Indeed there is no reason . . . You are so wonderful each day . . . Of every month and season . . . And as you give yourself to me . . . I give my love to you . . . And in the presence of our God . . . I promise to be true.

Armistice Day was declared to commemorate the end of World War I, at a time when we thought it had been the war to end all wars. The soldiers who died thought so, too. But war came again. Now Armistice Day is for all those who died then and who have died since, in the service of our country. Yet we believe in freedom and—

WE PROMISE THEM

Today our hearts commemorate . . . The dead of World War I . . . But all our prayers are equally . . . For every fallen son . . . For every son and daughter in . . . Our fight for liberty . . . Whatever battle of the year . . . Or of the century . . . We honor them and offer them . . . Our deepest gratitude . . . And promise that no tyranny . . . Will conquer or intrude . . . That no one will invade our land . . . And take away our rights . . . Or change our lofty principles . . . By lowering our sights . . . We promise them our courage and . . . Our faith to carry on . . . Until we win and there is peace . . . In every night and dawn.

A discussion is good, but an argument is seldom worth while, unless as a formal debate, with proper and restrained conduct on all sides. Why should we get hot under the collar when we disagree on something? Besides—

WE MIGHT BE WRONG

Let's not get overheated when . . . We have an argument . . .
Let's try to keep our tempers down . . . At least to some extent
. . . No matter what the issue or . . . How strongly we may feel
. . . About a certain thought that holds . . . Particular appeal . . .
There is a possibility . . . That we are very wrong . . . No matter
how we think some minds . . . Incline to go along . . . Of course
we have the right to say . . . Whatever words we please . . .
However much the Congress or . . . Our neighbor disagrees . . .
But why pursue an argument . . . As loud as it is long . . . When
no one really knows, and our . . . Opinion may be wrong?

Soap is both a necessity and a luxury. We have to have it to keep ourselves and our surroundings clean. On the other hand (well, both hands, to be exact) it is a luxury in the sense that we are fortunate to have this cleansing material, especially the scented kind. We should be grateful for all forms of—

SOAP ~ *good*

It comes in dry and liquid form . . . In powder and in flakes
. . . And with attractive wrappers it . . . Is shaped in bars or cakes
. . . One kind is for the dishes and . . . The laundry and the floors
. . . And one to scrub the working hands . . . When finished with
their chores . . . Milady likes the scented stuff . . . And then
there is the type . . . That bubbles in the bathtub or . . . Is bubbled with a pipe . . . Another is for leather goods . . . To make
them look more lush . . . And that which serves the daily shave
. . . Without or with a brush . . . But whether it is dry or wet
. . . Or white or pink or green . . . It is the welcome article . . .
That helps the world keep clean.

"Amen I say unto you, as long as you did it for one of these, the least of My brethren, you did it for Me." This quotation applies not only to acts of charity but also to wrongful deeds. Whether you help or hurt your fellow men, you are doing the same to God. You do unto Him—

✓ AS YOU DO UNTO THEM

When you offend a relative . . . Your neighbor or a friend . . . Then you are hurting God much more . . . Than ever you intend . . . For as you hurt your fellow man . . . By anything you do . . . So will He feel it in His heart . . . And lay the blame on you . . . Because He gave your soul to you . . . To live your life for others . . . That all the world might honor Him . . . As sisters and as brothers . . . And as you give your love to them . . . You give your love to God . . . And you will be rewarded for . . . Your place upon this sod . . . So live according to His way . . . And keep a kindly heart . . . For as you live for others, you . . . And God will never part.

The greatest heritage that we can leave our children is not money, fame, heirlooms or other worldly possessions. It is the gift, by example and teaching, of all the virtues they need to serve God and save their souls. If they received no more, they could not be richer in—

THEIR HERITAGE

I hope to leave a heritage . . . To my dear children three . . . A heritage of faith and trust . . . And love and loyalty . . . A heritage of faith in God . . . And trust in other souls . . . Of love for all, and loyalty . . . To all our country's goals . . . I pray that they will have the strength . . . And courage to go on . . . However dark and long the night . . . However dim the dawn . . . This is the only heritage . . . Of which I am concerned . . . That they may grow and profit by . . . The lessons I have learned . . . Then if I die in poverty . . . And leave them not a cent . . . I still will feel my time on earth . . . Was well and richly spent.

*It is beautiful and inspiring when those who are married remain
faithful to each other to the very end. And it is a wonderful feeling
for them on that silver or golden anniversary, as they say to each
other: Thank you—you have been—*

SO TRUE TO ME

You promised me with all your heart . . . As long as I might live
. . . That I would always have your love . . . As much as you
could give . . . It mattered not how dark the night . . . Or miser-
able the day . . . Or if a sudden tragedy . . . Should interrupt
our way . . . You vowed that you were mine alone . . . And you
would follow me . . . Along whatever path I took . . . Unto eternity . . . And now the years have disappeared . . . And I must
say to you . . . That you have kept your promise and . . . You
have been good and true . . . And now I only wish that I . . .
Could fully thank you, dear . . . And let you know how much my
heart . . . Has always been sincere.

*Some friends seem to have a sixth sense. They may not write or
call you often, but they always seem to get in touch with you at just
the right time—just when you need them most, or when you are
most hungry to hear from them. Such a person is truly a—*

WONDERFUL FRIEND

I have a friend who seldom writes . . . Or calls me on the phone
. . . And yet he always seems to know . . . When I am all alone
. . . He seems to know when I am sad . . . And need a helping
hand . . . And never fails to comfort me . . . Or fails to under-
stand . . . He has an intuition that . . . Is deep within his heart
. . . However long since we have met . . . However far apart . . .
I only wish that I could be . . . As wonderful a friend . . . To
everyone I say hello . . . Or any message send . . . I only wish
that I could be . . . As faithful and as kind . . . To every friend
I treasure and . . . Each new one that I find.

*We should all be sorry for our sins and mistakes, and we should
keep them in mind, as we resolve not to commit them again. But we
should not brood over them and condemn ourselves to the point
where we may lose our courage in the continuing struggle to live a
better life. It is good to regret, not so to dwell in—*

REMORSE

Remorse is not a pleasant mood . . . Of any night or day . . .
And we can do without it as . . . We go along our way . . . It is
that period of life . . . When all of us regret . . . Our sins, mis-
takes and errors that . . . We wish we could forget . . . Of course
we should be sorry for . . . The wrongs that we have done . . .
And all the clouds that we have caused . . . To keep away the sun
. . . But we can criticize ourselves . . . And carry it too far . . .
Until we tell ourselves that we . . . Are weaker than we are . . .
And then we lose our courage and . . . Ability to win . . . Because we are so sorry that . . . We finally cave in.

*There was a time when there was a motto on the wall of almost
every home—a slogan, a bit of advice. Not much in evidence today,
it served a good purpose, if only by its suggestion to live right, love
our neighbor, or ask God to bless our home and our guests. We can
always use a good—*

✓ MOTTO

A motto is an axiom . . . A proverb or a saw . . . A saying that
is serious . . . But not enforced by law . . . It is a guide to better
life . . . Upon a moral plane . . . And it can be a cozy roof . . .
Against the wind and rain . . . Sometimes on pretty parchment it
. . . Is hung upon the wall . . . And sometimes every word is read
. . . And sometimes not at all . . . Yet every motto does some good
. . . If only seen or heard . . . According to the counsel and . . .
The wisdom of each word . . . So let us listen closely and . . .
Behold each work of art . . . That every worth-while motto now
. . . May penetrate the heart.

good

Our life may not be an open book, but it surely is a book—in the hands of God. He does not write in it. We do that ourselves, with every thought and word and deed. Let us take care, then, what we record on—

OUR PAGES OF LIFE

Our pages all are numbered and . . . We have to fill them in . . . With every action in our life . . . Of charity or sin . . . We do not know how large the book . . . According to our age . . . Or what will be the number of . . . The last and final page . . . But it will be an accurate . . . Account of what we do . . . Including all the sufferings . . . We actually go through . . . So let us strive to write each page . . . According to God's way . . . As we pursue our life on earth . . . And live from day to day . . . Let us endeavor to correct . . . Our errors of the past . . . And write and live each coming page . . . As though it were our last.

November 21

There may be nothing significant about the time and place where we meet the one with whom we fall in love, but it seems sort of special when it happens at church. That was not my experience, but I know at least one happily married couple whose faces light up when they tell you—

WE MET AT CHURCH

I saw you on the avenue . . . In sunshine and in snow . . . I wished that I could follow you . . . Wherever you would go . . . I did not know you by your name . . . Until we met that day . . . As both of us went into church . . . To kneel and humbly pray . . . I looked at you, you glanced at me . . . And then we knelt and prayed . . . And in the presence of our God . . . We lingered and we stayed . . . And both of us were asking Him . . . To grant the same request . . . That we might really be in love . . . And be forever blest . . . And with the answer to our prayer . . . That ended every search . . . We thanked Him that we fell in love . . . As we went into church.

Surely you have experienced the anxiety and relief that accompany the disappearance and safe return of someone you cherish. You wait, you wonder, you worry, and perhaps you start a frantic search. And then you nearly burst with joy when that someone is—

SAFE AT LAST

There is no happiness in life . . . More wonderful or great . . . Than being with the ones you love . . . When they arrive so late . . . When you expected them to ring . . . Or knock upon your door . . . An hour or a day ago . . . Or anytime before . . . It may be just your neighbor or . . . A person far away . . . Or it could be your children on . . . An outing for the day . . . You wonder and you worry and . . . You hope and pray and wait . . . And finally you see their smiles . . . When time is growing late . . . And then you hug each other in . . . The morning or the night . . . And by the grace of God you know . . . Your loved ones are all right.

No score in sports is really important, nor is the worldly score we make in the game of life. It is not the outcome that counts but how we play the game. God will reward our honest efforts—the only thing it takes—

TO REALLY WIN

In football, baseball, basketball . . . Whichever game you choose . . . What does it really matter if . . . You win or if you lose? . . . Of course you want to win the game . . . And you will really fight . . . You do the very best you can . . . And that is only right . . . But why be disappointed if . . . Your score turns out too low? . . . There will be other contests in . . . The sunshine or the snow . . . It does not matter what they write . . . In any history book . . . But only how you struggled and . . . The courage that it took . . . Just do your best and give your all . . . In every game you play . . . And you will be the winner in . . . The true, important way.

*Every now and then we ought to check up on what we are doing—
in business and pleasure, and in our social and moral life. It is good
to take stock of ourselves and everything around us. Merchandise
and profits may diminish, our friends may fade from view, and we
may lose sight of ourselves unless we have—*

INSPECTION TIME

Inspection time is check-up time . . . And it is mighty good . . .
For office, home and government . . . And every neighborhood . . .
It takes an inventory of . . . The way we live our lives . . . And
whether one is negligent . . . Or he sincerely strives . . . It keeps
the soldier on his toes . . . It ferrets out the flaws . . . In business
operations and . . . The value of our laws . . . It offers an incen-
tive to . . . Be eager and alert . . . If only to protect the home . . .
From fire and from dirt . . . Inspection should be frequent and
. . . As thorough as can be . . . For health, protection, progress
and . . . The best economy.

*How big is your turkey? How large is your family? How great is
your gratitude to God for these and all the other blessings He has
given you? Before you eat, bow your head and say—*

WE THANK YOU, GOD

We thank You, God, for everything . . . That we possess today
. . . And most of all we thank You for . . . Our democratic way
. . . The right to live in liberty . . . And freedom from all fear . . .
In comfortable security . . . And brotherhood sincere . . . The
right to vote the way we want . . . And worship as we please . . .
According to our principles . . . And human sympathies . . . We
thank You for Your blessings and . . . The turkey that we eat . . .
And ask that You will hear our prayers . . . As humbly we entreat
. . . And thank You, God, for all Your gifts . . . However old or
new . . . We love You and we worship You . . . And give our
thanks to You.

We cannot make a wrong decision in life if we ask God to guide us, provided our prayer is sincere and fervent in faith. Things may not seem to turn out right at first, but they will eventually. We are bound to win if we tell Him: We place our trust—

IN YOUR GUIDANCE

I ask Your guidance, God, in each . . . Decision that I make . . . That I may never live this life . . . For my own selfish sake . . . I want to weigh my every move . . . And analyze its worth . . . According to the lasting good . . . That it may do on earth . . . Because I know that as I try . . . To do Your holy will . . . There is no hope or dream or prayer . . . That You will not fulfill . . . There is no evil power that . . . Can conquer or prevail . . . There is no test or trial true . . . That I shall ever fail . . . And so my each decision, God . . . Whatever time or place . . . Is one where I appeal to You . . . For guidance and for grace.

A happy marriage, like success in business or in any undertaking, is not accomplished overnight. It has to develop a day at a time. If your marriage is happy, you know that is true, as you thank your sweetheart—

FOR ONE MORE DAY

Good night, my love—God bless you, dear . . . For one more happy day . . . I thank you for your faithfulness . . . With words I cannot say . . . I thank you with my heart and soul . . . And every breath in me . . . Today, tonight, tomorrow and . . . For all eternity . . . I thank you for the kindness and . . . The patience you have shown . . . And every moment of our lives . . . Together or alone . . . For all the truth and courage and . . . The hopes that I possess . . . To live my life for you, my love . . . And bring you happiness . . . I cannot find the fitting words . . . But solemnly I pray . . . That God will always bless you in . . . His own and special way.

"No man can serve two masters." There is no loyalty unless it i
whole and complete. You cannot pledge it with any mental reserva-
tion. Loyalty must be absolute. It must be given—

TO ONE ALONE

You can divide your worldly goods . . . Your love and sympathy
. . . But in no righteous way can you . . . Divide your loyalty . . .
For loyalty is something pledged . . . To one and only one . . .
Until the promise is fulfilled . . . And every deed is done . . . It
may be loyalty to God . . . With every breath of life . . . Your
country, your employer or . . . Your children and your wife . . .
Wherever and however long . . . There must be binding ties . . .
Without a reservation or . . . The slightest compromise . . . No
matter how ingenious or . . . How clever you may be . . . You
can not serve two masters with . . . Complete fidelity.

True and lasting wealth is not to be found in worldly goods but
in the spiritual things of life, such as the friendship and brother-
hood of our fellow men. How easy it is to increase that wealth—
simply by cultivating new and worth-while friendships! Every time
I make another friend I feel I have become—

A RICHER MAN

My wealth increased today although . . . I did my best to spend
. . . I am a richer man—because . . . I made another friend . . .
I might have gained in stocks and bonds . . . I might have earned
more pay . . . I might have been the lucky one . . . To win a
prize today . . . But I bought sundry things with cash . . . And
paid some dusty bill . . . And now the balance in my bank . . . Is
little more than nil . . . And yet I am much wealthier . . . Than
I could ever be . . . As much as any worldly wealth . . . Is weighed
financially . . . Because I found a friend today . . . Who did not
stop to look . . . To see how much I carried in . . . My earthly
pocketbook.

Many modern conveniences provide added comfort and privacy,
but there is one old-time instrument that still serves a useful and
happy purpose, and that is the rural phone. It may not afford much
privacy, but in a rural community seclusion is not exactly in style.
And there are those certain, important times when we are mighty
grateful for that—

RURAL PHONE

The rural phone is quite the same . . . As it was years ago . . .
Where every message is the one . . . That all the neighbors know
. . . It is a widespread party line . . . Where any kind of ring
. . . Will keep the folks from all around . . . Informed on every-
thing . . . Of course there is a certain ring . . . For every country
phone . . . But when you hear and answer it . . . You never are
alone . . . There is no privacy, and yet . . . In those communities
. . . It is a life preserver when . . . There are emergencies . . .
For as the neighbors listen in . . . They hurry to your side . . .
And you are grateful that your voice . . . Was carried far and wide.

December 1

When the first day of December appears, we suddenly realize that
another year is drawing to a close. It is not just another month on
the calendar—it is the final one—the one in which we contemplate
the other eleven, and think back over all the years. December is our—

REMINDFUL MONTH

December days are here again . . . How swiftly goes the year!
. . . It is not any time until . . . The months all disappear . . .
What happened to the months of May . . . And June and January
. . . As well as August, April, March . . . July and February? . . .
And so it went through autumn and . . . Into the winter days . . .
The moments turned to memories . . . To go their separate ways
. . . There is no month or year on earth . . . That can go on for-
ever . . . But it is just a period . . . Of trial and endeavor . . .
. . . us do our very best . . . And always be sincere . . . We
hen it will be . . . Our final month or year.

We were not put upon this earth to live for ourselves alone, or for our loved ones, but for all the world. And whatever good we may do should be carried on by our children. Accordingly, we should teach and guide them, for the welfare of humanity. They are—

OUR FINAL HOPE

Our children are the jewels that . . . Our hearts should treasure more . . . Than any other thing in life . . . To make a higher score . . . For they behold our trials and . . . They witness our mistakes . . . And they have time to choose between . . . The angels and the snakes . . . As much as now we guide them and . . . We teach them right from wrong . . . The way to meet emergencies . . . And how to get along . . . They are the final hope we have . . . For peaceful life on earth . . . Where every human may attain . . . A goal of greater worth . . . So let us live for them today . . . And set examples true . . . That they may live and carry out . . . The things we tried to do.

A diary is not too difficult to keep, unless it is a diary of love, because then there may not be pages or ink sufficient to record your affectionate thoughts and feelings. And then you have to keep the rest of them in your heart, to speak for you when you say again: I want—

TO LET YOU KNOW

Tonight I held you in my arms . . . Tonight I said to you . . . Whatever fortune may befall . . . I will be ever true . . . And now I think it over as . . . I start to go to bed . . . And tell my diary the thoughts . . . That fill my heart and head . . . But as I make this record of . . . Each sentiment and sigh . . . I turn the little pages and . . . My fountain pen runs dry . . . I do not have sufficient ink . . . To write this memory . . . Of all the honeyed happiness . . . That you have given me . . . The other words are in my heart . . . And, oh, I hope they'll do . . . To let you know how very much . . . I am in love with you.

God does not compromise. There is only one way to get to Heaven, and that is to obey His commandments. There is no "time off for good behavior" to partake of sinful pleasure. There is no side road or detour of self-indulgence. The path to God is strictly a—

ONE-WAY STREET

The path that leads to Paradise . . . Is just a one-way street . . . And only those who worship God . . . Will pass His judgment seat . . . There is no short-cut and there is . . . No way to go around . . . The regulations and the rules . . . By which our lives are bound . . . We must obey the laws of God . . . In spirit and in sense . . . And for each sin that we commit . . . There must be recompense . . . We cannot swerve from side to side . . . Or try another shoe . . . Except as we may promise God . . . To start our life anew . . . There are no politics or bribes . . . Where finally we meet . . . The only path to Paradise . . . Is just a one-way street.

Did you ever feel frustrated? It is that feeling that no matter what you do or how hard you try, you cannot accomplish a certain thing— that everyone and everything seems to be against you. It is also a form of inferiority complex. Don't let your confidence be destroyed by—

FRUSTRATION

Frustration is that futile thing . . . That hides ourselves away . . . And keeps us from accomplishing . . . What we should do today . . . It is the secret notion that . . . We ought to be real great . . . Or anyway that we deserve . . . A more important state . . . Frustration is a demon that . . . Is sitting in our chair . . . And constantly is trying hard . . . To get into our hair . . . But if we take the time to think . . . That all of us are brothers . . . And in the manner that we live . . . We are just like all others . . . There will not be the complex of . . . Inferiority . . . But we shall live our lives on earth . . . In perfect harmony.

Millions of Christmas cards and packages go out in the mails every year, and almost without exception, they arrive at their destinations safely and on time. And the cost of mailing is so little! Sometimes we ought to say—

THANK YOU, P.O.

This time of year our Uncle Sam . . . Should smile from coast to coast . . . With all his first class profits and . . . The ones from parcel post . . . The packages and greeting cards . . . That everybody sends . . . To please the business customers . . . Or relatives or friends . . . And no one knows that better than . . . My family and I . . . With all the messages we mail . . . And bundles that we tie . . . But we are deeply grateful to . . . Our Uncle Sam today . . . For his efficiency and for . . . The little that we pay . . . His profit may be quite a bit . . . In terms of quantity . . . But ours is more in service and . . . In true economy.

Pearl Harbor Day is one we should never forget. We may "forgive and forget," insofar as our former enemy is concerned, but we must never forget our failure to be prepared for sudden infamy and treachery. The next time we relax or hesitate in our decision, it may be too late. Let us be always—

ON GUARD

However much our wounds are healed . . . And time has passed away . . . Let us remember in our hearts . . . It is Pearl Harbor Day . . . Let us remember what it means . . . In terms of treachery . . . But not with any hatred of . . . Our former enemy . . . Pearl Harbor is a lesson that . . . We never should forget . . . If we would live in peace on earth . . . And have no deep regret . . . It is the lesson that we must . . . Be constantly awake . . . And on our guard against the friend . . . Who may be just a snake . . . Whatever cost in taxes or . . . In other sacrifice . . . Our freedom and security . . . Are always worth the price.

Today is our wedding anniversary. I could not begin to put on these pages all the thoughts of love and gratitude I have for my dear wife and mother of our children, especially after more than twenty-five years of happiness together. Instead, here is her message and mine to all devoted husbands and wives—

GOD BLESS YOUR DAY

God bless the day that you were wed . . . In love and sympathy . . . And bless you more each time you have . . . An anniversary . . . As you abide together and . . . Remain forever true . . . You live your happy married life . . . As He would have you do . . . And as you bring some children forth . . . A darling girl or boy . . . May every moment multiply . . . The sweetness of your joy . . . God bless each sacrifice you make . . . Each moment spent alone . . . And comfort you as those among . . . The ones who are His own . . . God bless you every day and night . . . And most especially . . . When you embrace each other on . . . Your anniversary.

Whenever I think of my wonderful friends, I thank God for them, and I ask Him to bless them for the faith, comfort and encouragement they give me. Truly they are—

MY FRIENDS IN GOD

Of all the gifts and benefits . . . Where every rainbow ends . . . I thank my God with all my heart . . . For giving me my friends . . . What could I do without their smiles? . . . How could I get ahead . . . Unless I had their faith and hope . . . To keep me comforted? . . . Unless they gave me courage and . . . I had their praises too . . . And I could always tell myself . . . That they are really true? . . . They are the inspiration of . . . My life from day to day . . . And may I be of help to them . . . Along our earthly way . . . And as I cherish all my friends . . . Wherever they may be . . . May God be always good to them . . . And sometimes think of me.

The faithful old candle has not lost its charm or its practical purpose of providing light. Indeed it now has a sister in society, all dressed up in pretty designs and colors, to decorate the mantelpiece or festive board. The fancy candle is attractive, but the plain, unadorned kind is still—

MY CANDLE

Of all the candles, I prefer . . . The ordinary white . . . That glows inside a window like . . . A guardian at night . . . There are a thousand candle kinds . . . And I am quite aware . . . That some are works of gorgeous art . . . And some are really rare . . . As flowers or as animals . . . A tree or Santa Claus . . . Or other image out of wax . . . That merits some applause . . . But I prefer the simple kind . . . That burns by night or day . . . And not the sculptured snowman who . . . Must slowly melt away . . . I like the lowly candle as . . . I kneel beside my bed . . . Or at the altar of my God . . . I humbly bow my head.

No other prayer is so sweet and simple as that which flows from the lips of a little child. It is so sincere and believing that it surely touches the heart of God. If only we could recapture those moments! If only we had the words and the feeling once more—

TO PRAY AS A CHILD

I wish I were a child again . . . And I could really pray . . . As fervently and simply as . . . The words I used to say . . . I wish I had the innocence . . . That once belonged to me . . . That I might give myself to God . . . In all sincerity . . . There is no gift more pleasing to . . . Our Lord and God above . . . Than just the adoration and . . . The praise of childish love . . . The little eyes that turn to Him . . . And try to see His face . . . And ask His heart to bless them with . . . His everlasting grace . . . I wish I were a child again . . . So sweet and pure and whole . . . But I must pray to God that He . . . Have mercy on my soul.

We always want to be with the one we love, but there are those special moments and hours when we need that someone more than at any other time. We long desperately for the comfort and courage that no one else can give us, as we implore—

I NEED YOU NOW

This night I want you more, my love . . . Than you will ever know . . . Not just because of circumstance . . . Or how the wind may blow . . . Not just because of promises . . . That you and I have made . . . Or anything that might disturb . . . Or make our hearts afraid . . . But just because it is the time . . . I want to be with you . . . When no one else upon this earth . . . Can do the things you do . . . I need the comfort of your arms . . . The laughter on your lips . . . And all the courage of the men . . . Who brave the sea in ships . . . I want you more, I need you more . . . Than time and destiny . . . Because you are the only one . . . Who means so much to me.

Yes, wisdom comes with age, but that does not mean it cannot be present in youth. Sometimes we are inclined to ignore or belittle the efforts of younger persons simply because of their tender years. Yet some of our greatest achievements have come from the young. Unless we give them a chance, how shall we ever know—

HOW WISE IS WHO?

How old are we at 17? . . . How old at 34? . . . And when we get to 51 . . . What is the actual score? . . . Is age the greatest factor in . . . This life we have on earth? . . . And must we live for many years . . . To prove our solid worth? . . . The older people seem to think . . . That wisdom comes with age . . . Though many victories appear . . . Upon the youthful page . . . I am in favor of the young . . . I do not want to wait . . . To hear their views until they reach . . . The age of 68 . . . And if I keep my heart and mind . . . And live to 85 . . . I'll thank the thoughts of 17 . . . To keep myself alive.

When you get married and have children, you naturally want to live your own life, in your own surroundings. But don't forget or neglect your parents. Pay them a visit now and then. They must be lonely without your presence, and it will make you happy, too, to say—

HELLO TO MOM AND DAD

When you are grown and married and . . . You have your family
. . . You like to stay at home and share . . . Each other's company
. . . But also it is pleasant and . . . It makes for moments glad . . .
To pay a visit just to say . . . Hello to Mom and Dad . . . They
may be living right in town . . . Or many miles away . . . But
when you knock upon their door . . . It is their happy day . . .
Because they love you and adore . . . Your children one and all
. . . They think of you and always they . . . Are hoping you will
call . . . So keep them in your hearts and when . . . You have
some time to spare . . . Be sure to visit Mom and Dad . . . And
show them that you care.

What matters the weather if you are in love? It may be raining or hailing, but in your heart the sun is shining, and there are stars in your sweetheart's eyes. You tell your loved one—

YOU ARE MY WEATHER

You make my life so wonderful . . . There is not any room . . .
For loneliness, discouragement . . . Or any kind of gloom . . .
Each day is happy from the start . . . With sunshine in the sky
. . . Despite the cloud the weatherman . . . May say is drifting by
. . . Each night is beautiful with stars . . . And with a moon of
gold . . . No matter what the experts and . . . Their instruments
have told . . . As long as you are mine, my love . . . The weather
cannot change . . . And in the magic of our world . . . There is
no picture strange . . . Because you are my sunlight and . . . The
silver stars that shine . . . And day and night are wonderful . . .
As much as you are mine.

A calendar is more than just a compilation of days and weeks and months. It is our reminder of those special occasions when we honor someone or something, from New Year's Day to Christmas Morn, including family birthdays and anniversaries. That is the really important answer to the question—

WHY A CALENDAR?

What good is any calendar . . . With months and weeks and days . . . Unless it has a meaning true . . . According to our ways? . . . Unless we honor Washington . . . The Pilgrims and the others . . . And all who now are true to us . . . As sisters and as brothers? . . . Unless we live as Christians and . . . We honor Christmas Day . . . And share the world with race and creed . . . In all our work and play? . . . Dear Mother's Day and Easter are . . . Among the dates we treasure . . . And those that give the calendar . . . Its more important measure . . . A calendar is filled with dates . . . But none holds anything . . . Unless we honor and respect . . . The meaning it may bring.

No one has ever benefited from telling a dirty or off-color joke. Any such storytelling lowers one's moral stature, and it may seriously harm the wholesome thinking of the listener. Let us keep a—

CLEAN TONGUE

What is our measurement of joy . . . As jokes are told today? . . . Are we at all compelled to tell . . . The ones that are risqué? . . . Why don't we stick to sayings that . . . Are clean and wholesome fun? . . A child's remark, a slip of tongue . . . Or some ingenious pun? . . . There is no true excuse on earth . . . For any dirty story . . . And while some folks may laugh, it makes . . . A lot of others sorry . . . We may be really interested . . . In cheering up a pal . . . But if we tell those tales we are . . . Destroying his morale . . . So let us live with innocence . . . In everything we mean . . . To join our thoughts with God and keep . . . Our conversation clean.

We may ask God's help in surviving our trials and attaining our goals, but we should never ask Him to remove all obstacles from our path, or to accomplish our task for us. He wants us to fight our own battles, with His grace and guidance, and to win our way to Heaven. So let us pray: Give us—

YOUR GUIDING GRACE

Dear God, we do not ask of You . . . That all our troubles end . . . Or that You give us all the help . . . And power You could send . . . We know that we must fight our way . . . As bravely as we can . . . And live according to Your word . . . With every fellow man . . . But we need inspiration, God . . . And perseverance too . . . And so we ask Your guiding hand . . . With special grace from You . . . We do not have the stamina . . . That guarantees success . . . And we might flounder in the tide . . . Of sorrow or distress . . . We need Your blessing and we ask . . . That You will lead us on . . . In peace and love and charity . . . To Your eternal dawn.

What was it that first attracted you when you fell in love—the sparkle of a pair of eyes, or their wistful gaze? Was it the touch of a hand, or perhaps the sound of a voice? More often the answer is—

I LOVE YOUR VOICE

Your voice is like a golden song . . . That has a soft refrain . . . As spring would whisper to the trees . . . Beneath a gentle rain . . . It is a melody of love . . . That lingers in my heart . . . Long after I have left your side . . . And we are far apart . . . I hear its echo in the dawn . . . And when the sun is high . . . Until the silver of the stars . . . Is all around the sky . . . Your voice is like a magic wand . . . That makes my dreams come true . . . Because I know inside my soul . . . That it is really you . . . And just to be with you, my sweet . . . Is paradise to me . . . Oh, let me listen to your voice . . . For all eternity.

Our friends can do so much to help us through life. Even on the darkest day—in the sky or in our souls—they can lift up our spirits and make us feel that, after all, it is worth our while to go on and fight the good fight. Sometimes so much—

DEPENDS ON FRIENDS

However bright or dark the day . . . Where life begins and ends . . . There is the consolation and . . . The joy of having friends . . . The comforting advice from those . . . Of long and many years . . . The sentimental happiness . . . Of all their smiles and tears . . . Because we live together and . . . We never are alone . . . As long as we are neighbors and . . . We love them as our own . . . In their companionship we learn . . . The lessons of this life . . . Including all the ways to meet . . . Our struggle and our strife . . . And so whatever path we take . . . It frequently depends . . . Upon the influence of those . . . Who want to be our friends.

Life may never be as wonderful as we hope and dream, but neither is there much chance that it will ever be as tragic as we fear. Then why not take life in stride and do the best we can, instead of worrying over—

OUR PROSPECTS

What are our prospects in this life . . . We live from day to day? . . . Our chance to gather happiness . . . Or sorrow on our way? . . . Well, prospects never are as good . . . As all our hopes and dreams . . . Nor do they really spell success . . . For our ingenious schemes . . . And yet they cannot ever be . . . As bad as all our fears . . . So why be worried now, and why . . . Resign ourselves to tears? . . . Our prospects are no more in life . . . Than possibilities . . . So why should we consider them . . . As cold realities? . . . Our prospects are the visions that . . . Pursue our heart today . . . According to the choice we make . . . Along our daily way.

Winter is the fourth of God's wonderful seasons. We may not like the weather it brings, but there is the beautiful snow that draws happy laughter from the lips of little children, and there is Christmas, and then New Year's, and Valentine's Day. We have every reason to—

THANK GOD FOR WINTER

Thank God for winter here again . . . With cold and rain and snow . . . That help the fields where later on . . . Our daily bread will grow . . . Thank God for sleds and stocking caps . . . Toboggan slides and skis . . . And all the forests beautiful . . . With fragrant Christmas trees . . . For chimney smoke and fireplace . . . Our warm and cozy beds . . . And Santa Claus with shiny toys . . . For little sleepy heads . . . It is the time to contemplate . . . The moments that are past . . . And promise that the new year will . . . Be better than the last . . . Thank God for winter and for all . . . The blessings at our door . . . Be glad for every season and . . . Give praise forevermore.

When you have a canary or parakeet in your home, it requires some daily time and effort to care for such a bird. But when you feed and water the birds of the air—the ones that linger on your window sill—all you need are a few bread crumbs and, somewhere on your lawn, an inexpensive—

BIRDBATH

We have a birdbath out in back . . . Near where the sidewalk ends . . . To give a bit of comfort and . . . To please our feathered friends . . . And every day they fly in there . . . To drink and splash around . . And then they skip away and search . . . For crumbs upon the ground . . . We know that they enjoy their bath . . . Because they chirp and sing . . . And we can hear their laughter in . . . The flutter of each wing . . . And even in the wintertime . . . We do our best to please . . . By making certain every day . . . The water does not freeze . . . It does not cost a penny for . . . The pleasure it extends . . . And we are always happy to . . . Invite our feathered friends.

The love of spouse for spouse always seems to take on a special meaning at Christmastime, and well it should. As we think of The Holy Family, we feel more and more the warmth of human love, and we are drawn closer to each other in the bond of carrying on God's design of creation on earth. Our love becomes our—

CHRISTMAS LOVE

I love you everywhere we go . . . Whatever place or clime . . . But somehow you mean more to me . . . When it is Christmastime . . . I love you every season and . . . Each month of every year . . . And every day in every way . . . You seem to grow more dear . . . But Christmas is that special time . . . When you belong to me . . . Not for this moment, darling, but . . . For all eternity . . . Because it is the hour when . . . That little Child was born . . . Our Jesus and our Saviour on . . . That wondrous Christmas Morn . . . And as I bow before my God . . . And as I humbly pray . . . I love you more than ever, Dear . . . On this His Christmas Day.

Christmas is that beautiful, wonderful, holy day of the year when we commemorate the birth of Jesus Christ, The Son of God. May His blessing be always upon you and yours, especially—

THIS CHRISTMAS MORN

God bless you in the hour of . . . This holy Christmas Morn . . . When we commemorate the day . . . His only Son was born . . . May He be with you in your home . . . To love and comfort you . . . And give you all the grace you need . . . In everything you do . . . May He protect the ones you love . . . However near or far . . . And guide their souls to Bethlehem . . . Beneath His brilliant star . . . And when another year begins . . . According to His will . . . May He be always at your side . . . And all your prayers fulfill . . . God bless you on this Christmas Day . . . And every gift you give . . . And bless you every hour and . . . Each moment that you live.

*Each year we poor husbands know it's coming, and yet we cannot
avoid it or even prepare for it. We wish there were some way out—
even to run away and join the French Foreign Legion—but there is
just no escape from that—*

DAY AFTER CHRISTMAS

The morning after Christmas Day . . . Should be a happy one
. . . We all enjoyed our presents and . . . The children had their
fun . . . But now I have to catch the bus . . . And go to work
again . . . And slave and toil throughout the day . . . With all my
fellow men . . . My wife is burdened with her tasks . . . And with
those extra chores . . . Including gifts to be exchanged . . . At
certain local stores . . . The house looks far from being like . . . A
palace to display . . . With every room and everything . . . In
utter disarray . . . And now and then I seem to get . . . The fever
and the chills . . . That magnify and multiply . . . The stack of
Christmas bills.

*Did you ever sit and dream before the burning logs of a fireplace
in winter, when flames cast their shadows about the room? Your
thoughts blend with the shadows, and they become the ghosts of the
past. You do not dwell on the present or future. You think only of
what is gone. Slowly you fall asleep with your—*

MEMORIES IN WINTER

I like a cozy fire on . . . A chilly winter night . . . While in my
favorite easy chair . . . I ponder and I write . . . And as the
shadows glide and dance . . . Upon the floor and wall . . . There
are a thousand things in life . . . I silently recall . . . The sunshine of the summer and . . . The snows of yesteryear . . . The
hand I held, the face I touched . . . To kiss away a tear . . . The
many miles of travel and . . . The people that I met . . . And all
the merry moments that . . . I never could forget . . . And in the
thousand memories . . . That are my own to keep . . . I dream
before the fireplace . . . And slowly fall asleep.

at are calling cards? They are bits of stiff paper, with plain or
printing, or embossed pieces of parchment. Their purpose is to
duce the business caller, leave a reminder, or make a social im-
ion. They usually serve their purpose, but there are other and
more effective—

CALLING CARDS

There are a lot of calling cards . . . Of plain or fancy kind . . .
To introduce, to advertise . . . Or simply to remind . . . Embossed,
engraved or printed flat . . . With color or without . . . They are
the representatives . . . Of those who move about . . . Sometimes
they merely give the name . . . The Mr. and/or Mrs. . . . Sometimes the phone and the address . . . And just what business this is
. . . Though I have not the prominence . . . To have them made
for me . . . I do enjoy the ones I get . . . And their variety . . .
But more than all the costly ones . . . That people can conceive
. . . I love the calling cards that are . . . The handshakes I receive.

What would you do if you knew that this would be your last day
on earth? Probably you would spend the entire time trying to make
amends for all your wrongs. But you cannot know in advance, so why
not live today as though it were the last? Why not consider—

EACH DAY THE LAST

Lord, let me live my every day . . . As if it were my last . . .
And strive to make amends for all . . . The sins that fill my past
. . . Let me be kind to everyone . . . In thought and word and
deed . . . And share what worldly goods I have . . . With those
who are in need . . . Help me, O Lord, with strength of heart . . .
And with Your holy grace . . . To walk in calm and patience and
. . . To keep my humble place . . . I want to be Your servant, Lord
. . . And always do Your will . . . Until my eyes are closed in
sleep . . . Until my heart is still . . . Be merciful to me, O Lord
. . . For my imperfect past . . . And let me live my every day . . .
As if it were my last.

Some families keep their Christmas trees until New Year's; others toss them out the day after Christmas. In either case, the tree is gone too soon, and empty is the room where it stood. If only it stayed there from day to day, throughout the year! We could have an—

ETERNAL YULE

I see the pretty Christmas trees . . . That decorate the town . . . And wish the folks who put them up . . . Would never take them down . . . Because it leaves an emptiness . . . That stares us in the face . . . And there is nothing like the tree . . . That ever takes its place . . . It seems to hold the spirit and . . . The warmth of Christmas cheer . . . For which my heart has hungered through . . . The hours of the year . . . Its branches are the loving arms . . . That touch the friendly wall . . . And bear the fruits of merriment . . . And kindliness to all . . . If only people would not throw . . . Their Christmas trees away . . . The world could make believe that it . . . Was Christmas every day.

The old year is dying now, but it will never really die. It will remain alive in our memory forever and ever. Our successes and failures, our joys and disappointments, our smiles and our tears—all will linger in their lasting effect on our life. Let us thank God for the past, and implore His help for the future, as—

THE EMBERS FADE

The glow of dying embers lights . . . Our little living room . . . And there are shadows on the wall . . . Without a shade of gloom . . . As we are sitting here tonight . . . To contemplate the year . . . Upon the calendar that is . . . About to disappear . . . The days and months of happiness . . . The dreams that all came true . . . Our sacrifices and, of course . . . Our disappointments too . . . We made some worthy progress and . . . Our children grew and learned . . . And what we have acquired now . . . We feel that we have earned . . . And as we watch the embers fade . . . Inside our fireplace . . . We say a fervent prayer to God . . . For guidance and for grace.